Page to Stage

Edited by Mike Gould

HEINEMANN PLAYS

Heinemann Educational Publishers
Halley Court, Jordan Hill, Oxford OX2 8EJ
Part of Harcourt Education

Heinemann is the registered trademark of
Harcourt Education Limited

© Harcourt Education Limited, 2004

First published 2004

08 07 06 05 04 03
10 9 8 7 6 5 4 3 2 1

British Library Cataloguing in Publication Data is available
from the British Library on request.

ISBN 0 435 23337 8

Typeset by 🔺 Tek-Art, Croydon, Surrey

Printed in the UK by Clays Ltd, St Ives plc
Cover photo: © Corbis

Tel: 01865 888058 www.heinemann.co.uk

Contents

Chapter 3: Scriptings: Understanding script production – from stage to performance

Chapter 4: Interpretations: Exploring different effects and perspectives

Chapter 5: Reflections: Analysing and commenting on drama

Acknowledgements

Every effort has been made to contact copyright holders of material reproduced in this book. Any omissions will be rectified in subsequent printings if notice is given to the publishers.

Extract from *Cyrano De Bergerac* by Edmond Rostand, published by Carcanet Press. Reprinted by permission of Carcanet Press Limited. Extract from 'The Listeners' by Walter de la Mare, from *The Complete Poems of Walter de la Mare 1969* reprinted by permission of The Literary Trustees of Walter de la Mare and the Society of Authors as their representative. Hollywood Words and Music by Madonna and Mirwais Ahmadzai © 2003 Webo Girl Publishing Inc, USA and 1000 Lights Music Ltd (50%) Warner/Chappell North America Ltd, London W6 8BS(50%) EMI Music Publishing Ltd, London WC2H 0QY. Reproduced by permission of International Music Publications Ltd All Rights Reserved. Extract from article 'Time of your life: three people record their day – Father Bellenger' from *Real Time Supplement/The Guardian 29ᵗʰ June, 2003* © Carl Wilkinson, June 2003. Used with permission. Extract from *Spoonface Steinberg* by Lee Hall, published by Methuen. Reprinted by permission of Methuen Publishing Limited. Extract from *Billy Liar* by Keith Waterhouse and Willis Hall, first published by Michael Joseph 1960. Copyright © 1960 Waterhall Productions Limited. Reproduced by permission of The Agency (London) Limited. All rights reserved and enquiries to The Agency (London) Limited, 24 Pottery Lane, London W11 4LZ info@theagency.co.uk. 'How Crazy are Those Who Love You So Much' by Kishwar Naheed, translated by Mahmood Jamal, from *Urdu Poetry* edited by Mahmood Jamal, published by Penguin Books in 1986. Reprinted by permission of Mahmood Jamal. Extract from *Golden Girls* by Louise Page, published by Methuen in 1985. Reprinted by permission of Methuen Publishing Limited. Extract from *Eastenders* script by Tony Jordan 12ᵗʰ November, 2001. Copyright © Tony Jordan. Reprinted by permission of Bill McLean on behalf of Tony Jordan and the BBC. Extract from *Ernie's Incredible Illucinations* by Alan Ayckbourn, published by Faber and Faber. Reprinted by permission of Sir Alan Ayckbourn and Faber and Faber Limited. Extract from *Eclipse* by Simon Armitage published by Faber and Faber. Copyright © Simon Armitage. Reprinted by permission of DGA (David Godwin Associates) on behalf of the author. Extract from *Mariza's Story* by Michele Celeste, published by Heinemann. Copyright © Michele Celeste. Reprinted with permission of the author. Extract from *Sparkleshark* by Philip Ridley, published by Faber and Faber. Reprinted by Faber and Faber Limited. Extract from *My Mother Said I Never Should* by Charlotte Keatley, published by Methuen in 1988. Reprinted by permission of Methuen Publishing Limited. Extract from *Blood Brothers* by Willy Russell, published by Methuen. Reprinted by permission of Methuen Publishing Limited. Extract from *Stone* by Edward Bond, published by Methuen in 1976. Reprinted by permission of Methuen Publishing Limited. Extract from *Rosencrantz and Guildenstern Are Dead* by Tom Stoppard. Copyright © 1967 by Tom Stoppard. Reprinted by Faber and Faber Limited. Extract from *East is East* by Ayub Khan-Din. Reproduced by permission of The Agency (London) Limited. All rights reserved and enquiries to The Agency (London) Ltd © Ayub Khan-Din 1996, 1997 first published by Nick Hern Books, 1996 all rights reserved and enquiries to The Agency (London) Ltd, 24 Pottery Lane, London W11 4LZ fax 020 7727 9037. Extract from *Ti-Jean and his Brothers* by Derek Walcott. Reprinted by permission of Farrar, Straus and Giroux, LLC. 'Black Truth' by Brenda Agard, from *Watchers and Seekers*. Copyright Brenda Agard. Reprinted with the kind permission of the author. 'Richard III' by John Thaxter, found at www.thestage.co.uk reprinted with the kind permission of the author. 'Come on Baby, Light my Fire' by Dominic Francis, written for The National Theatre Education Department's magazine, *StageWrite* and featuring on the National Theatre Website. Reprinted by permission of National Theatre. Review of film *Drive me Crazy*. Reviewed by 'The Wolf' on IOFilms website. Reprinted with the kind permission of 'The Wolf' and IOFilm, Stobo Hopehead. Extract from an interview with Barnaby Kay, found on Ambassador Theatre Group website. Interview with Shane Richie, found on *Eastenders* website www.bbc.co.uk/eastenders. Reproduced with permission of the BBC.

Introduction to the student

Whether you remain seated in your chair or are leaping around a drama studio, you need to see *all* the drama texts you read and study from a performance perspective.

You need to be able to consider how an actor or actress would prepare a particular role; you need to be able to analyse your own understanding of character, action and theme – whether as actor, director, or audience member. You need to be able to see inside the mind of the playwright and answer such questions as 'What did he or she intend?' 'What is he or she saying about this issue?' 'What effect was he or she attempting to create?' Even 'What is the tradition or convention behind this drama?'

This book will help you answer these questions. It provides you with a wide range of scripts – from ones written many centuries ago, to radio and television dramas of recent years. As you read and study the scripts, imagine them in performance, as they lift off the page and take life on the stage or screen.

Drama lives and breathes, and if you can see these texts in this way, rather than as lines and directions on a white sheet of paper, you will gain a great deal, as much in developing your own dramatic skills and techniques as in understanding the skills and techniques of others.

Introduction to the teacher

Page to Stage is designed to provide a wide range of source material for use in the classroom or drama studio, in support of the Framework for Teaching English's drama objectives, and the Drama Objectives Bank. This is done by providing a structured yet flexible resource which focuses on the key skills of:

- Collaborations – working together to make drama
- Repertoires – focusing on individual and group drama techniques
- Scriptings – exploring the craft of writing drama
- Interpretations – developing the skills of the directorial perspective
- Reflections – learning how to comment on, and analyse, drama work.

Each of these chapters contains a range of source texts. The majority of these are scripts; however, Chapter One provides a number of images, fragments, prose and verse texts, designed to stimulate improvised, devised and scripted work.

Each source text or extract has an accompanying set of activities and tasks ranging from text-based, interpretative study through to more practical, active learning. In addition, each chapter ends with an extended task, or set of tasks, relating to one or more of the texts studied. The format for the activities follows that recommended in the Drama Objectives bank – namely: *Making, Performing, Responding*, though these do not always occur together within the text (i.e. the last chapter has, not surprisingly, a greater number of '*responding*' tasks).

In essence, however, this is a collection of stimulating and challenging source materials, designed for you to use in whatever way you see fit, but assembled into broad categories for ease of use.

Chapter 1: Collaborations

At the heart of drama is collaboration. This is what happens when people work together to create a dramatic experience. Even at its simplest level – one actor performing, one watching – a collaboration takes place. Performer and audience enter a shared space. This section is about how you can work together to make dramatic experiences come to life. It starts by showing you how even tiny fragments of text, or images, can suggest ideas for drama.

In this chapter you will:
- improvise drama from a range of texts and images
- discover how a group can work together to help ideas develop
- learn about polished improvisations
- use dramatic techniques such as 'tableaux', 'soundscapes' and working in role.

Images and objects

What follows is a range of images. It is sometimes helpful to bring real objects to drama lessons – an old biscuit tin, a broken mobile phone, a baseball cap, a recording of a strange tune, and so on. These objects can stimulate ideas, and make you consider stories and dialogues. Look at the images below, and as you do so, interrogate them – what can be seen? What is happening (if anything)? How did the people/objects get there? What is the story behind the image? Use the activities on pages 19–20 to help you.

Lines spoken

Words, too, are like images. They can suggest stories, hide truths, reveal lies.

They also raise questions: Who is speaking? What came before these words? What comes after? What is the attitude of the person writing or speaking? Where did these words happen? As you look at these fragments, think of all the possibilities for story-telling and drama they suggest to you. The way they have been divided is not set in stone. Ending lines can also be starters, and vice versa. Use the activities on page 21 to help you.

Starters

I've brought you something …

Dad, I have something to tell you …

Look, I'm really sorry, but I have to ask you this …

Look: the beach is empty …

Lines anywhere

It's unbelievable!

You're lying.

Right – let's have a look.

I'm sorry – I can't.

Lines ending

Everything's abandoned! Destroyed!

You won't see me again.

Just remember what I said.

It'll be our secret.

It's your choice.

I can hear the sirens.

Look at the moon!

I'm sorry – I can't wait until then.

Fragments

Various sources

Longer chunks or extracts from texts can also be a good place to start when developing dramatic ideas. You don't even have to use the actual text in your piece, but you might come up with ideas about what had led up to this section in a story, or who might be speaking these lines, and then take your drama from there. Read through the extracts and fragments below before looking at the activities on pages 22–23.

My Dear Maclise
  You will be greatly shocked and grieved to hear that the Raven is no more. He expired to-day at a few minutes after Twelve o'Clock at noon. He had been ailing (as I told you t'other night) for a few days, but we anticipated no serious result, conjecturing that a portion of the white paint he swallowed last summer might be lingering about his vitals without having any serious effect upon his constitution.

We were first equal Mary and I
with the same coloured ribbons in mouse-coloured hair …

'Is there anybody there?', said the Traveller,
Knocking on the moon-lit door …

… the isle is full of noises,
Sounds and sweet airs, that give delight and hurt not…

FRANKIE	You didn't actually kill her, did ya, Jake?
	(Jake stays seated. Starts slow, low deliberate.)
JAKE	She was goin' to these goddamn rehearsals every day. Every day. Every single day. Hardly ever saw her. I saw enough though. Believe you me. Saw enough to know somethin' was goin' on.
FRANKIE	But you didn't really kill her, did ya?

The Listeners

Walter de la Mare

Sometimes, a whole text is used as a stimulus for drama activity. Look at the well-known poem below. It tells the story of a traveller who arrives at a house in the moonlight. Not much more happens – but an atmosphere is evoked, and lots of possibilities are suggested. Who are the 'listeners'? Why is the traveller 'lonely'? Could these questions be answered by a piece of drama, or could the poem suggest a new story? As you read the poem, think about the possibilities for a piece of drama, then do the activities on page 24.

'Is there anybody there?' said the Traveller,
    Knocking on the moonlit door;
And his horse in the silence champed the grasses
    Of the forest's ferny floor:
5 And a bird flew up out of the turret,
    Above the Traveller's head:
And he smote upon the door again a second time;
    'Is there anybody there?' he said.
But no one descended to the Traveller;
10   No head from the leaf-fringed sill
Leaned over and looked into his grey eyes,
    Where he stood perplexed and still.
But only a host of phantom listeners
    That dwelt in the lone house then
15 Stood listening in the quiet of the moonlight
    To that voice from the world of men:
Stood thronging the faint moonbeams on the dark stair,
    That goes down to the empty hall,
Hearkening in an air stirred and shaken
20   By the lonely Traveller's call.
And he felt in his heart their strangeness,
    Their stillness answering his cry,

While his horse moved, cropping the dark turf,
        'Neath the starred and leafy sky;
25 For he suddenly smote on the door, even
        Louder, and lifted his head: –
    'Tell them I came, and no one answered,
        That I kept my word,' he said.
    Never the least stir made the listeners,
30   Though every word he spake
      Fell echoing through the shadowiness of the still house
        From the one man left awake:
    Ay, they heard his foot upon the stirrup,
        And the sound of iron on stone,
35 And how the silence surged softly backward,
        When the plunging hoofs were gone.

The Traveller

Polished group improvisation

A polished improvisation usually means a piece of improvisation that starts with an immediate response to a stimulus, such as 'The Listeners', but is then refined and reworked to create a new piece. Usually, though not always, no script is written down, and the piece develops organically as the group works on it. In this example, a small group of students read the poem 'The Listeners' and took the first line from it, and some of the ideas that appeared in it. As you will see, however, there the similarities end. Use the activities on page 25 to help you.

Characters in order of appearance (4)

The Traveller
Voice
Older Man
Smithy

THE TRAVELLER	Is anybody there?
VOICE	*(offstage)* No.
THE TRAVELLER	There must be somebody.
VOICE	I'm nobody.
5	*A small, thin figure enters.*
THE TRAVELLER	Come into the light.
VOICE	The light hurts.
THE TRAVELLER	Are you sick?
	There is no reply.
10 THE TRAVELLER	*(moves to centre stage)* I need water.

VOICE	*(suddenly)* Water?
THE TRAVELLER	*(gently)* For my horse.
	Older man enters.
OLDER MAN	Who are you?
15 THE TRAVELLER	A traveller.
VOICE	He wants water.
OLDER MAN	Everyone needs something.
THE TRAVELLER	I'll go.
VOICE	Let him stay! He may have news.
20 OLDER MAN	Are you alone?
THE TRAVELLER	I have a companion. *(calls)* Smithy!
SMITHY	*(enters)* Yes, master?
THE TRAVELLER	Is the horse well?
SMITHY	*(sadly)* The horse has gone.
25 THE TRAVELLER	He'll return. Come into the light.
SMITHY	I don't want to.
OLDER MAN	Let us see you.
	Smithy moves into the light.
VOICE	*(gasps)* Father!
30 OLDER MAN	Can it be true?
THE TRAVELLER	Yes.
OLDER MAN	But he lives?
SMITHY	I am well.

OLDER MAN	But the marks?
35 **SMITHY**	They are only marks.
THE TRAVELLER	Come into the light, child …

Voice comes closer.

SMITHY	Like me!
OLDER MAN	*(sighs with relief)* You are not alone, child.
40 **VOICE**	I can't leave.
THE TRAVELLER	Smithy left.
OLDER MAN	He travels with you?
THE TRAVELLER	We cannot stay long in any one place. Ignorance breeds fear. We must move on. But we live in the 45 world, not outside it.

Voice moves close to Smithy and touches his lips and neck with the tips of her fingers.

OLDER MAN	Your water. *(He passes him a vessel)*
THE TRAVELLER	Come, Smithy.

50   *Smithy hesitates, then starts to leave.*

VOICE	*(suddenly)* I want to go!
OLDER MAN	You cannot!
VOICE	Why not?
OLDER MAN	Look at you.
55 **VOICE**	I am no different from him.

Older man considers this. He moves to the corner of the room and picks up a hat and bag.

OLDER MAN	We will leave together.
THE TRAVELLER	There is another place five miles down the road. There are moonlit fields, dark streams. A fire burns in the hearth.

They move away. Older man turns and shuts the door.

VOICE	Look at the moon!
THE TRAVELLER	We live while it burns.
OLDER MAN	Let us reach the house before day comes.

They leave.

Fade up the light, then sudden blackout.

Hollywood

Madonna and Mirwais Ahmadzai

Some of the best drama can arise from looking at well-known icons, or by listening to music – from any source. One particularly effective drama activity is to look at a day in someone's life. This can be someone famous, like Madonna, or someone who does an unusual job, or someone whose life is ordinary. These song lyrics from Madonna's album, *American Life*, convey the need of people, especially in the USA, to 'make it' – that is, to become famous, especially in films, music or television. Madonna, who has made it in all these fields, probably feels particularly able to comment, especially as she has now left to live in London. As you read the lyrics, think about how this might inspire a piece of drama set in Hollywood. Then complete the activities on page 26.

Everybody comes to Hollywood
They wanna make it in the neighbourhood
They like the smell of it in Hollywood
How could it hurt you when it looks so good?

Chorus:
5 Shine your light now
This time it's got to be good
You get it right now, yeah
'Cause you're in Hollywood

There's something in the air in Hollywood
10 The sun is shining like you knew it would
You're riding in your car in Hollywood
You got the top down and it feels so good

Everybody comes to Hollywood
They wanna make it in the neighbourhood
15 They like the smell of it in Hollywood
How could it hurt you when it looks so good?

I lost my memory in Hollywood
I've had a million visions, bad and good
There's something in the air in Hollywood
20   I tried to leave it but I never could

There's something in the air in Hollywood
I've lost my reputation, bad and good
You're riding in your car in Hollywood
You got the top down and it feels so good

25   Music stations always play the same songs
I'm bored with the concept of right and wrong

Everybody comes to Hollywood
They wanna make it in the neighbourhood
They like the smell of it in Hollywood
30   How could it hurt you when it looks so good?

(Chorus)

'Cause you're in Hollywood
'Cause you're in Hollywood
In Hollywood *(repeat twice)*

(Spoken)
Check it out, this bird has flown

Recording my day: the monk

Father Aidan Bellenger

This is part of an article that looks at how different people spend their days. It is certainly very different from the life that Madonna describes in 'Hollywood'. In this account, Father Aidan Bellenger, Prior of Downside Abbey in Somerset, describes a typical day. As you read it, think about what you would be doing at the same times. How close is your life to his? And, if you were acting out his day, how would you convey its order and (mostly) peacefulness? Then complete the activities on page 27.

05.30 Wake up, shave and wash in preparation for a bell that rings at 05.40 calling us to prayer.

06.00 We have a service in the church called *vigils*. Because we all have jobs, we don't get up to pray during the night.

5 **06.30** Private prayer and meditation.

07.00 *Lauds* – the first morning service. It's a rather cheerful service to greet the morning.

07.30 Breakfast, where we read the newspapers or any letters that have arrived.

10 **08.45** Mass for all the monks. This is in Latin, and full of Gregorian chants. One monk gives a short sermon.

09.15 As prior, I head to my office to see any of the monks who need money or permissions – basically permission to leave the abbey. It's just a courtesy thing really.

15 **11.00** Coffee with visitors.

11.30 I work in the monastery library, where I'm writing a historical article. I write a lot of ecclesiastical history.

13.10 Midday office. Short prayers.

13.15 Lunch is our main meal of the day. We eat in silence while
20 somebody reads. After, I talk to the Abbot about business, then
return to my office to make phone calls.

14.30 Walk in the grounds of the Victorian abbey.

15.00 Snooze in my room.

16.00 See some of my parishioners on pastoral matters.

25 **16.30** Cup of tea.The abbey has a boys' boarding school and I
usually walk over to check their library is in order.

17.45 Vespers, or evening office. Again a rather jolly service.

18.15 Spiritual reading in my room or private prayer.

18.45 A light supper.

30 **19.10** Recreation in the common room where all the monks have
a chat or read.

20.00 Compline or night office.This service is held in the dark
without candles and the Abbot blesses the community. Then
there is silence until the following morning.

35 **23.00** Bed.

---

compline last service of the day

Activities

Images and objects (page 4)

Making

There are many different ways of developing drama from a picture or photo. Here are some ideas for you to try out.

1. 'Activating' the image

This works best with people, though it can work with objects, landscapes, etc.

Bring the photos on page 5 to life by adopting the positions of the people in the image. Try to get as close as you can to the expressions, stances and overall 'feel' of the image.

If the image is from the past, it can be interesting (though time-consuming) to try to find similar clothes and objects.

Once you have 'activated' the image in a frozen moment, you can:

- bring it to life – the characters start moving, speaking
- rewind – discuss and work on what happened just before the image was taken
- fast forward – look at a later scene involving some or all of the people in the image.

You can, of course, simply use the image as a starting-point for a piece of drama that is only vaguely related to what is going on. For example, if the image shows a storm, perhaps you could develop a story based on the effects of a storm.

2. The secret object

Objects make for great drama. On their own, they create speculation.

A key: where is it from? Who owns it? What does it unlock? Where will it lead to? Will it be a gateway to joy, sadness, hate, love, despair?

Look at the objects on page 4. They are on the page, of course, but try the following:

Sit in a circle. Imagine the object placed in front of you. If possible, one of you could 'pick it up' and pass it round, having felt its texture, shape, etc. You can make comments: they might be based on what can be seen in the image, or they might be invented.

Student A: It's heavy!

Student B: It's dirty.

Student C: Yuk! Here – you have it!

Student D: What's this? An engraving!

Student E: A name, I think.

Lines spoken (page 6)

Words, like images and objects, can spark all sorts of ideas in your mind and lead to interesting ideas. But, first, it's useful to try out the sound of the words, feel them on your tongue, investigate their possibilities. It's amazing how a simple line can take on all sorts of meanings once you try it out several times.

Making

1. In pairs, take **one** line or phrase from the 'Starters' section on page 6. Say it to each other in as many different ways as you can, *stressing* different words. For example:

   'I've brought you *something*' might suggest that the thing I'm giving is not great, but better than nothing.

   '*I've* brought you something' might suggest that at least I gave you something even if no one else did.

2. Now try taking one line from the 'Lines anywhere' section on page 6 and try an instant dialogue with your partner. You don't have to start with the phrase, but you must include it somewhere in a ten-line conversation.

   A Open the door.
   B You do it.
   OK – if I have to. You go in.
   B Everything's abandoned! Destroyed.
   A Err … it's not our house.

Performing

Now try a more extended improvisation. At random, take any line or sentence from any of the three sections on pages 6–7, and depending on whether it is a 'starter', an 'anywhere line', or an 'ending', develop a short dramatic piece (no more than a minute or two long) that uses the line. Try not to 'block' your partner's work by throwing the idea away, or introducing a silly idea that kills the drama.

Responding

When you have finished, discuss five *other* directions your drama could have taken from your chosen line (no need to come up with new performances).

Fragments (page 8)

A good deal of the drama you will do, will spring from more than just single lines or words. An imagined scene, or larger image, can lead to ideas, narratives and themes.

Making

1. Create a *circle dialogue*: in groups, stand in a circle. One person (or two if it's the dialogue) stands in the middle. They select a line from one of the extracts and fragments from page 8, and speak it to the group. Then the person in the centre asks questions about themselves, e.g.

Person/s in middle	*Who am I?*
Group member	*You are an old lady on her last voyage.*

   Once some details have been established, discuss as a group what the story behind these lines might be. Once the simple story is established, the group tells another group the story, one person taking a line at a time.

2. Now tell the story as a series of five tableaux (frozen pictures or sculptures), not using words. Each tableau will represent a different part of the story.

Performing

Perform the five-stage simple story in tableaux to the class, or another group. Can they identify which was the original inspiration from the fragments list?

You may wish to do a second performance, in which one simple line from the story accompanies each tableau. For example:

Tableau:	old woman looking out over 'sea'
Line:	I remember my childhood friend

Responding

Take the germ of the story your group worked on, and turn it into a longer piece of writing. Write in the first person, from the point of view of someone in the story. Add new ideas, or alter elements of the story in any way you wish.

The extracts in this section were written by:

- Charles Dickens (a letter to a friend)
- Liz Lochhead ('The Choosing')
- Walter de la Mare ('The Listeners')
- William Shakespeare (*The Tempest*)
- Sam Shepard (*A Lie of the Mind*).

The Listeners (page 9)

Longer works – stories, poems, songs, etc. – can be turned into powerful staged dramas. One example is Henry James's short, haunting novella, *The Turn of the Screw*, which has been turned into an opera, stage play, and film.

Making

1. Read 'The Listeners' aloud, either on your own, or sharing lines with a partner or members of your group. Then consider these questions:

- What actually happens (if anything) in the poem?
- Who is 'the traveller' and why do you think he came to the house?
- Who are 'the listeners' and why do they remain silent?

2. Re-read the poem. Select a powerful phrase or line (e.g. *phantom listeners*) and say it out aloud several times until you know it by heart. Then, in a group, create a *soundscape* where you each say your line/phrase in turn, perhaps repeat it several times, to create a hypnotic, growing chant. The group must decide when to stop.

Performing

Next, in your group, take the first line from the poem: 'Is anybody there?' and try a spontaneous (instant) improvisation that leads from this point. The only constraints are that it must involve:

- someone who is rather spooky or threatening arriving at a house
- the person who knocks does not leave (immediately) and something happens (good or bad).

Responding

When you have finished, consider what sort of dramatic impact you created. How can you now, in your group, *refine* (make better) what you did?

- take the elements that worked well, and keep them
- alter – or remove – the elements that didn't work.

Now run the improvisation again with your changes.
Was it more effective? Was the impact stronger?

The Traveller (page 11)

This is a transcript of a polished improvisation that developed out of work on the poem 'The Listeners' on pages 9–10. Read through the transcript carefully and then look back at the original poem. See if you can identify which elements have been kept by the group who devised the improvisation, and which elements have been changed. Then work through the activities below.

Making

Divide up the parts in *The Traveller* and either read through or work through a rough performance of the transcript.

The original poem 'The Listeners' was quite haunting, and had a certain sadness to it. Have you been able to keep this in your first attempt at performing the transcript?

If not, discuss ways you can make the piece carry that feeling of threat, of doom … of sadness, too.

Do you need to consider the roles of the various speakers? How should they speak? How should they move?

Performing

Perform *The Traveller* a second time, trying to incorporate some of the changes you have discussed. This time, don't use the script at all, but just use it as a base for your own improvisation. You can keep the basic story and idea, but the actual words can change. Remember: this was not a written script originally – it is just a record of how the group performed.

Responding

When you have finished, discuss the following questions:

- How different was your version from the transcript you started with?
- What advantages were there to working *without* the transcript in your hands?
- What disadvantages?

Hollywood (page 15)

It is increasingly true that anyone who releases a pop song, releases a video with it. Indeed, in many cases the video is shown before the song actually goes on sale. Many videos simply showcase the singer or band performing, but most try to tell a story of some sort – a kind of mini-drama.

Making

Read Madonna's song, 'Hollywood' on pages 15–16, either aloud or to yourself. Then, take each of the lines below and draw a quick sketch (as if from a pop video) to go with each one. There must be a person in each image. Think about why people go to Hollywood, and what dangers there might be to their physical (and mental) health.

Everybody comes to Hollywood   *SKETCH: girl getting out of taxi with case*

The sun is shining, like you knew it would

I've had a million visions, bad and good

I tried to leave it but I never could

Once you have these pictures, make simple 'sculptures/tableaux' of each one.

Performing

One person reads the whole song aloud. As they get to the selected lines above, the group – or individual – moves into the position (tableau) for each line.

Alternatively, play the actual song , and perform the four tableaux.

Responding

Now discuss in your group, how you could take what you have done further:

- If you are making a drama/play – what story does the song suggest? What might happen?
- If you are creating a dance – what new moves could you add or develop from the tableaux you have created?

Recording my day: the monk (page 17)

This lifestyle is very different from the one portrayed in 'Hollywood'. What sort of drama could develop from the day described here?

Making

Dramas tell stories, and every day of your life is a kind of mini-story.

On your own, perform a mimed routine, in which you act out the events of a typical day in your own life from the moment you wake up, to the moment you leave your house to go to school.

Think very carefully about the *gestures* you use. In particular, slow all your movements down, so it is absolutely clear what you are doing.

Now look again at Father Bellenger's day on pages 17–18. Choose *one* moment from it (e.g. walking in the grounds, working in the library) and work on how Father Bellenger might move and behave in this section. Keep the piece as a mime.

Performing

Perform your 'mini-mime' as if you are Father Bellenger. If you wish, you can join up with other group members and put your mimes together to create 'a day in the life of a monk'.

Responding

There is a calm and order about the monk's day. If this were to be developed into a piece of drama, some form of complication or problem would need to arise.

What might that problem be, and how might it be resolved?

Consider the possibilities below, or one of your own, and discuss how a dramatic piece could be developed from them.

- one of the monks has doubts about his faith and wants to leave
- something of value in the monastery goes missing
- a bishop or cardinal comes to inspect the monastery, hearing that it is costing the church too much to keep up.

Development and extension

Collaboration

Collaboration is about seeing possibilities. Even with simple fragments or images, it is about where you can take that idea – what story it suggests.

Look at this response by one group of students to a simple object that was shown to them:

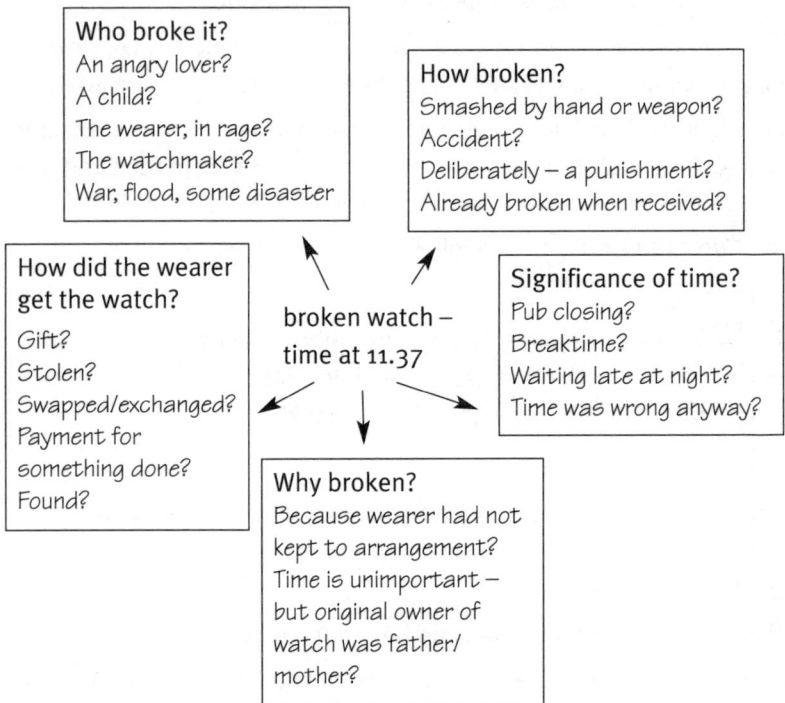

```
Who broke it?
An angry lover?
A child?
The wearer, in rage?
The watchmaker?
War, flood, some disaster
```

```
How broken?
Smashed by hand or weapon?
Accident?
Deliberately – a punishment?
Already broken when received?
```

```
How did the wearer
get the watch?
Gift?
Stolen?
Swapped/exchanged?
Payment for
something done?
Found?
```

broken watch –
time at 11.37

```
Significance of time?
Pub closing?
Breaktime?
Waiting late at night?
Time was wrong anyway?
```

```
Why broken?
Because wearer had not
kept to arrangement?
Time is unimportant –
but original owner of
watch was father/
mother?
```

Now create your own brainstorm either around a real object, or around an imaginary one from this list:

- a ring with the initials *S.S.* on it
- a withered bunch of flowers still inside their presentation wrapper
- a roll of film that has been exposed to the light so no images can be seen.

Once you have done your brainstorm, invent a simple scene in which the object is present. Decide:

- who is there
- what they are doing
- the significance (if any) of the object at this time
- what is going to happen next.

For example ...

Guest turning up for a wedding carrying a bunch of flowers. Met at door of church by bridegroom or someone else.

Developing your scenario

Next, take your initial idea and scene, and now develop your idea into a ten-point, complete story:

1	*Guest turns up for wedding carrying bunch of flowers. Met at door by bridegroom. He doesn't recognise guest, but someone else does ...*
2	*Flashback: 'Guest' is talking woman out of suicide attempt on bridge. Woman is 'bride'. She gets down.*
3	*Flashback: guest and woman in hospital. Woman says man saved her life.*
4	
5	
6	

Now take your whole story and share it with a group.

- decide on the best scenario/story and develop a piece of drama around it
- there is no need for a written script, and the piece may use music, mime, or any other format to tell the story.

Chapter 2: Repertoires

This chapter contains a wide variety of different scripts. From reading them and doing the activities that follow, you will be able to develop a range – or repertoire – of different skills for rehearsal and performance. These skills cover areas such as voice, movement and use of space.

In this chapter you will:
- read a wide range of scripts of different forms
- explore a variety of different performance styles (e.g. performing monologues, use of ritual, etc.)
- use a range of different vocal techniques (e.g. different types of voices for the same character, stressing different words, etc.)
- develop ideas about use of space and gesture.

Spoonface Steinberg

Lee Hall

This is an extract from a radio play by Lee Hall, who also wrote the script
for the hit film, *Billy Elliott*. This moving monologue, about a young
autistic girl, received thousands of calls to the BBC in its praise when it
was broadcast in the mid-1990s. In this extract, Spoonface reveals how
she got her name, and also how she came to know that she was different.
Read through the extract below, then complete the activities on page 54.

I was never right ever since I was born – this means that I do very
bad writing and that I can't speak proper and that I am backwards
and that I am a special child – but why is a mystery for what they
have not got an answer – but Mam said when I was born it was at
5 a dark night and it was raining and thundery and all the cats and
dogs and things were under the tables – and the wind was
screeching round everywhere – and everything was quite horrible
– but I didn't mind because I was just little and I was in the
hospital and Mam kissed me and when she looked at my face she
10 noticed that it was round – and everyone came and looked at my
face – and they laughed and said I was Spoonface because when
they looked at my face it was round as a spoon and when you
look into a spoon you see this face just like mine – and that is
how I came to be Spoonface Steinberg – because my other name
15 is Steinberg – but I never even knew because I was just a little
baby and all the stars and planets were moving inside of me and I
was looking up and the world was as bright as colours and as
shimmery as light and I was just a baby – and when you're a baby
you have a soft head and that – and that's what makes you
20 backwards. Sometimes when it's very late at night – when they
think I'm asleep, Mam says to Dad that maybe it is his fault that I
am not right – on the fact that on the day Dad came back when
he was out with the floozie, I did fall off the chair – Dad came
back and it was quite late for our tea and I was sitting on the chair

---

and Mam said that Dad was out with someone – and Dad says he was in the office doing the meeting – and Mam said she phoned the meeting and he was off with the office doing a floozie – and that this was one of his students – and she was going somewhere – off with the final straw – then there was all this crying and screaming and Dad went like a beetroot and Mam said that the student was just a baby and had big boobs and I fell over – it was like when you bump your head only worse – and then everything went white like lightning – and this was bad on account of my softness – and they were crying there with me and I was silent as a worm – and Dad told Mam he would not ever have another floozie if Mam would be nicer and Mam said she would be nicer – and then it was that everything was alright – except I started going backwards – but I am not sure if this is to do with it or not – maybe it is – maybe it is not – I think I was backwards before the fall – before Dad came back and everything – I think I was always backwards ever since I was born and there was all the thunder and that, and I think ever since I was born that my brain was quite special – I think I have a special brain what is quite different in how it was and stuff – but nobody knows for sure – all the experts with all their computers and all the doctors who poke in your ear and look into your brain and all the people who do the quizzes and all questioners and such like – none of them know for certain – they all said no one can know can ever know for certain – and that's what Dad says – he says there is only one thing for certain – nobody knows anything for certain – what is true I think – on account that he is a lecturer of philosophy – the thing is even now I am old I cannot read proper or to write and am very bad at games and that I cannot go to a proper school as I am not allowed on account of my brain – but I am quite a special little girl, though – that's what Mrs Spud says – Mrs Spud does the cleaning – and she says that I am quite one of the special girls she has ever known and every time she comes she brings me a sweetie which is very nice for she has so many problems of her own – she says that everybody is different and that it is quite good

60　indeed and that we should all be happy and that – for every person
　　is a very special person and that it is good to be different as if
　　there's no difference we would all be the same – and Mrs Spud told
　　me not to worry about my brain because to be different is to be
　　who you are – so I do not believe that I fell on my head – I do not
65　believe that I was affected – or it was Dad's fault for the floozie or
　　Mam's fault 'cos I was unattended – I believe that I was supposed
　　to be backward – I believe it was all part of what is supposed to be
　　– and when I was born God came and touched me on my head –
　　down he came and touched my soft spot and made me.

70　MUSIC　　　　　*Maria Callas singing 'Mon coeur s'ouvre à ta voix' from*
　　　　　　　　　　Samson et Dalila *by Saint-Saëns.*

　　One day I started to do the numbers. This was when Dad came
　　back from the university and he was with a calculator for doing
　　the marks. He was sat doing the marks when he said two
75　numbers and I went 42 – because it was the answer of the two
　　numbers – and then he goes – goodness me – and then he said
　　two more numbers and I said 147 – which was another answer –
　　and then he did more and more – and some of the answers he
　　had to do on the calculator – and then he started shouting of
80　Mam – and Mam came running as if there was something bad –
　　but it was only me doing the numbers and I did more and more –
　　and Mam kissed me and was crying and that – and Dad kept
　　doing more and more and he was laughing – and Mam said he
　　had to stop – and I said what was it that had made her cry? – and
85　she said that it was because of the numbers and never in the
　　world did they know I could do the numbers – but I could do
　　them now – and I was a genius – and it was of my brain.
　　　　And then I had to do them in front of a doctor – and then the
　　doctor said – if Spoonface can do numbers then she can do dates
90　– and then I did some – this is how I do it – what is the day of July
　　the 4th 2010? – Saturday – amazing, absolutely amazing – and that
　　is how I do the dates and they have to look it up in a book as
　　soon as I've said the answer and there it is – and they say how do

I know so many numbers? and I say I don't know – and how do I
know so many dates? – and I also say I don't know – but it's just
obvious like colours – and that is why – and Mrs Spud says that is
why we are all different – to me the numbers are obvious and to
her some other stuff is obvious – like how to clean the loo and
that – but at least that means we're all different.

So this is all because I am autistic – and that is quite a big strain
on Mam and Dad which was account of why they did split up – for
a start Mam was quite sad – she was in the house when Dad went
to work and she did look at her books and such like as she was
getting a **Ph.D** also like Dad – only he finished quicker on account
of women have to have babies that men can't have – this meant
that hers was much slower – and she would sit in the room and
when ever she was just to do some work I came in and then she
had to stop – and it wasn't fair of me to do the Ph.D – and Dad
was on the committees – so Mam had to drink the vodka – and
she used to sit with the book and the vodka – and Dad came back
and she said – that he was not of attention – and maybe he wasn't.

Then one day Dad said he had met one person who was doing
a different Ph.D to Mam and that she was very nice and that he
would go away to live with her for a bit – and Mam said she was
glad of him to go — and even though I was backwards and that –
it would be better than his stupid face – and off Dad went for a bit
until sometimes he came back for a few minutes on a Saturday.

Then Mam used to have more and more – and she would come
to me and say 'My poor sweet angel, my poor sweet angel' – and
then drink the vodka – and then she had to take tablets off the
Doctor and would stop the vodka at the same time – except one
time she had the pills and the vodka and went to sleep on the
stair and I put on her a nice blanket in case anyone tripped – but
nobody did trip as there was only me – then the next day Mrs
Spud came and tidied up where she had been sick.

Ph.D Doctorate of Philosophy – a high-level qualification, above a degree

Billy Liar

Keith Waterhouse and Willis Hall

Monologues can make up the whole of a drama (a sort of dramatised story-telling), but they can also occur within a play. They are usually used (as in Shakespeare's plays) to reveal a character's thoughts.

This extract concerns a young man, Billy Fisher, who lives at home and works for a local undertaker. He is engaged to two girls, Barbara and Rita, neither of whom is aware of the other's existence. Billy dreams of escaping his humdrum life, so makes his life more interesting by telling a string of lies to all the people around him. The pills referred to are 'passion pills' given to Billy by a friend, designed to make Barbara feel sexy (without her knowing). Read through the extract below, then complete the activities on page 55.

Barbara, picking up her handbag, crosses into the hall and goes upstairs.

Billy picks up her glass and crosses to the cocktail cabinet, where he pours out two more drinks. Taking the 'passion pills' from his pocket, he adds two pills to Barbara's glass and then, on impulse, he adds the
5 *entire contents of the bottle into her glass. He is standing admiring the glass and its contents as the telephone rings in the hall. He places the glass on the table and crosses into the hall where he picks up the phone.*

BILLY   The Fisher residence? Can I help you? *(His manner changes)*
Oh, hullo, Mr Duxbury. No, well, I'm sorry but I've had an
10   accident. I was just leaving for work and I spilt this hot
water down my arm. I had to get it bandaged.... Oh, well,
I think there's a very simple explanation for that, Mr
Duxbury. You see, there's a lot of those figures that haven't
been carried forward. ... I use my own individual system. ...
15   No. No, not me, Mr Duxbury. Well, I'm sure you'll find that
there's a very simple explanation. ... What? Monday
morning? Yes, of course I'll be there. Prompt. Thank you,
Mr Duxbury. Thank you for ringing. Goodbye, then.

(He puts down the telephone for a moment and is lost in
depression. He brightens as, in his imagination, he addresses
20   *his employer)* Well, look Duxbury – we're not going to
argue over trivialities. As soon as I've finalised my
arrangements with Mr Boon I'll get in touch with you. *(He*
picks up the telephone) Hello, Duxbury? ... I'm afraid the
25   answer is 'no'. I fully agree that a partnership sounds very
attractive – but frankly my interests lie in other directions.
I'm quite willing to invest in your business, but I just have
not the time to take over the administrative side. ... Oh, I
agree that you have a sound proposition there. ...
30   Granted! I take your point, Mr Duxbury. What's that little
saying of yours 'You've got to come down to earth.' It's
not a question of coming down to earth, old man. Some
of us belong in the stars. The best of luck, Mr Duxbury,
and keep writing ...

35   *He breaks off as Barbara approaches down the stairs.*

For her benefit, he goes into another fantasy as she passes him
and enters the living-room.

Well, Doctor, if the leg's got to come off – it's got to come
off... *(He replaces the telephone and looks speculatively at the*
40   *living-room door)* It's not a question of coming down to
earth, Mr Duxbury. *(He pauses)* Some of us, Mr Duxbury,
belong in the stars.

Billy, who has now regained his self-confidence, enters the
living-room and crosses towards Barbara with her glass of port.

45   *Curtain*

Alibi

Mike Gould

The following monologue is an entire short play. It shows how the
monologue form, as well as contributing to a play as a whole, can also
tell a complete story by itself. This play concerns a young man, Stephen.
The title and setting suggest a prison, and that Stephen is a criminal.
But is he? And what, if anything, has he done wrong? Read through the
extract below then complete the activities on pages 56–57.

Enter Stephen, small, skinny, about 14.
There is a single chair at a table. A light hangs low over it.
He sits. Looks over his shoulder.
There is a packet of cigarettes on the table.
5 *He picks up the packet; opens it.*
There's nothing inside. He tosses the packet down on the table.

STEPHEN   I'm not saying anything ...

Silence.

Not a word. Not to you. I know what your sort are like.

10   *He sits back in the chair, arms crossed. Defiant. A few seconds*
pass. He leans forward again.

And even if I did, you wouldn't believe me.

Let's face it, I could say anything. I could say I passed
your house today, and your wife was hanging the
15   washing out, and I blew her a kiss and she smiled and
laughed and ...

He sighs.

But it'd be rubbish. Not the bit about your wife and the
kiss. No, that could happen alright. No, the bit you
20   wouldn't believe would be me walking past your house,
right?

'Cos I'd never go near your house, would I?

Beat.

You know something?

25   The other day I was watching the telly and there was this ad for a car. It wasn't fancy or nothing. Had a family and countryside and a picnic. And just now I thought – that could have been you.

Course it was an actor and all that. But who knows?
30   'Cos that's your sort of life, I bet. All cosy and roses. All Persil washes whiter. That's your life. White. Clean. Not like mine.

Beat.

I don't know why I'm here. I'm an idiot.
35   Truth is, I should never have done it.

There, I've said it. I've actually said it. *I did it.* Yeh. It was me. No one pushed me into it. It was my decision. I confess.
Happy now, are you?

40   What? Nothing to say? Still – that's no surprise.
'Cos you've never let me speak before. Never heard my story.

You know something? This all goes back to a simple thing. This whole business. It's funny how one thing
45   can set it all off. Like a nudge in the back leads to a push, then a punch, then a kick, then a whole beating.

For me the nudge was the phone on the wall.
Just that. A phone.

All the other kids used it. Never me. Never had no one
50   to call.
Then one night, about three, I couldn't sleep. So, I slip out of my room. There was supposed to be someone

about, but they must have fallen asleep. All I wanted was a drink … Yeh, I know what you're thinking. No, not that sort of drink. Just some cold milk, or a coke. Whatever was in the kitchen.

So I go downstairs and into the hall. The floor's cold. There's no carpet – too difficult to clean up mess. I go to the kitchen but it's locked. I guess they reckon we can get at the knives and things. And I can be dead threatening with a wooden spoon.

Anyway, I'm about to go back up the stairs to my room when the phone in the hallway rings. It just rings. I stare at it. Wondering what to do.

I don't wanna get caught downstairs so I don't call out to the others.
It carries on ringing. Ring, ring. Like a drill.

And that's when it hits me.
What if this time it's for me? What if…?
Well, it don't matter because before I can think straight it stops ringing.

Like a fool I pick it up.
Like they do on TV.
And I stare at it, like they do on TV.

It's dead of course.

Stephen sighs, gets out of his chair. Takes several steps away from the table. Turns.

But that was the nudge. The start. That phone wouldn't stop ringing.
I kept on thinking. What if that call was for me?
'Cos until then I'd sort of blocked it out.
Like a crime I'd committed.
Like I was to blame.

But when that phone went I realised.

85 Realised that maybe you didn't know about me.

He sits again.

Of course I know now that it couldn't have been you.
You didn't know where I was.
Nobody told you and you didn't ask.

90 So. Here I am.
I'm in charge now.
Not used to that.

But I'm not gonna say nothing when you walk through
that door.

95 In two minutes' time when that door swings open I'm
gonna play dumb, which isn't difficult.
'Cos I know that the moment I open my mouth I'll start
confessing.
Saying like it was *my* fault.

100 Like I must have been really ugly.
Really difficult.
Wild.
Easy to get rid of.

No. I'm gonna let *you* do the talking.

105 I'll just sit back. Keep silent.
I'm good at that.

Yes Dad.
This time you can do all the explaining.
Tell me your alibi for the last fourteen years.

110 Tell me where you been, what you done.
And when you've stopped explaining.
When you're all explained out …
Then, Dad, I'll tell you what I think.

You can hear my story.

How Crazy Are Those Who Love You So Much

Kishwar Naheed (translated by Mahmood Jamal)

Poems are mini-dramas. Anyone who has heard poetry performed live will recognise how close it is to drama, in the way the poet communicates with the audience and tells them his or her story. Read the following poem, by the Urdu poet Kishwar Naheed, which could almost be a speech from a drama. What is the story around it? Who is she talking to? Look for the different voices in the poem. Use the activities on pages 58–59 to help you.

With words of chastity he adorned my hands,
chained my feet like prisoners,
and called it modesty.
How sweet and pleasant it sounds,
5 like a diamond,
like the gleam of a knife!
He says: 'What more can you ask for?
Walls of marble, clean and shining
to keep you safe. The gold lock and chain
10 on big, solid black mahogany doors
at least show that it's all for you,
for your security, for your love.'

How lovingly and hopefully built,
this home full of ideals and dreams!
15 It's been tested with screams,
making sure that if a sound
dare penetrate some crevice
it will turn to foam, exhausted,
and nothing will get through.

20 'Tenderly, for you, for your love
this home, this throne, these marble walls.
All for you, my dear,
all because I love you!'

Fear no more (from *Cymbeline*)

William Shakespeare

Two characters speaking in unison, or in partnership, can create powerful and dramatic moments on stage, whether in song or speech – or a combination of both. In this extract from *Cymbeline*, two brothers say these lines over the body of their dead sister (they don't know she's their sister, and, in fact, she's not dead, simply drugged). As you read or perform them, consider how the two actors can work together to make these lines moving or powerful. Use the activities on page 60 to help you.

Characters (2)

Guiderius
Arviragus

GUIDERIUS	Fear no more the heat o' th' sun
	Nor the furious winter's rages;
	Thou thy worldly task hast done,
	Home art gone and ta'en thy wages.
5	Golden lads and girls all must,
	As chimney-sweepers, come to dust.
ARVIRAGUS	Fear no more the frown o' th' great;
	Thou are past the tyrant's stroke.
	Care no more to clothe and eat;
10	To thee the reed is as the oak.
	The **scepter**, **learning**, **physic**, must
	All follow this and come to dust.
GUIDERIUS	Fear no more the lightning flash,

scepter symbol of royalty
learning education
physic medicine

ARVIRAGUS	Nor th' all-dreaded thunder-stone;
GUIDERIUS	Fear not **slander**, **censure** rash;
15 ARVIRAGUS	Thou hast finished joy and moan.
BOTH	All lovers young, all lovers must Consign to thee and come to dust.
GUIDERIUS	No exorciser harm thee,
ARVIRAGUS	Nor no witchcraft charm thee.
20 GUIDERIUS	Ghost unlaid forbear thee;
ARVIRAGUS	Nothing ill come near thee.
BOTH	Quiet **consummation** have, And renownèd be thy grave.

---

slander untrue and unkind words spoken about someone
censure criticism/punishment
consummation completion/ending

Golden Girls

Louise Page

Movement is a natural and fundamental part of any staged play. Even when there is only one speaker who remains seated throughout, there is gesture, eye movement, and so on. However, some plays have movement as an integral part of the story or the staging, and this can cause difficulties for director or producer. Read the following extract about a group of top international women runners preparing for a relay race, then complete the activities on page 61.

Characters in order of appearance (6)

Noel (Sue's father)
Sue
Laces (the coach)
Muriel
Pauline
Tom (a sports journalist)

It is early morning. Noel has been timing Sue's run, and is about to give her a one-minute break before she starts again.

NOEL One minute recovery.

SUE I hate running tired. Running with your mind, not your
5 body. Waiting for the moment when the two fuse.
Knowing that some days they won't. That all it will have
been is putting on your tee-shirt, your tracksuit. Tying
your laces. The routine. Other days the most perfect,
perfect thing. No thoughts at all. Absolute symmetry in
10 your head. Like the perfect races when you know just
what to do. Not yesterday, a ragbag of tactics and
strategy. I could feel the clock in my head. Time running
out. And knowing every fraction of a second that there
wasn't going to be a moment which lasted for ever.

---

15   *Noel shows her the time on the stopwatch.*

NOEL   Again.

SUE   No.

NOEL   I said again.

SUE   No.

20 **NOEL**   Don't take that tone with me, miss.

SUE   I can't better that.

NOEL   You can and you will.

         (Pause)

         You're a winner, love. You just have to get it together.

25   Then it won't be living in a camper for decent facilities.
         You'll have everything you deserve. A pretty girl like
         you, Sue. Think about it.

SUE   It's impossible.

NOEL   It's not, love. I've shown you it's not. You're a winner,

30   love. From the day you were born.

SUE   Don't throw that at me.

NOEL   You were a winner then.

SUE   Don't tell me that.

NOEL   She'd be proud.

35 **SUE**   Not listening.

NOEL   Me proud then. Crack it and you can stay in bed for ever.

SUE   Who wants to stay in bed in a camper?

NOEL   If you want everything they've got here.

         (Pause)

40   What do you want?

(She shakes her head)

We'll go home. I'll drive you twenty miles there and back everyday. But you still won't get the half of what they've got here.

45   **SUE**   I can't run any faster for you, Dad –

NOEL   Then run it for yourself. Come on. Again.

(She runs off. He watches her. Laces jogs back on)

She could have gold, couldn't she? Real gold.

LACES   There won't be anything if she over-does it.

50   **NOEL**   She wasn't allowed to run her own event without running the relay.

LACES   It's the same for all four of them.

NOEL   It's hardly the same amount of glory.

LACES   Muriel, Pauline, Dorcas, Sue – I'm not saying that
55   they're the most perfect team – yet.

NOEL   Certainly weren't yesterday –

LACES   But they could get so near. So exciting. Certainly be the best there's been in this country for a very long time. I know it's not peace and light between the four of
60   them but when they're on that track with the baton – they could be –

NOEL   I don't like the word perfect.

LACES   But nearly that. I don't want Sue to let it slip through her fingers. Not now they've come this far together.

65   **NOEL**   You don't think she's any good on her own?

LACES   She's superb.

(Noel is pleased)

That's why I need her in the relay. She's got that power for that first leg.

70   I know it's been hardest for her. That she's giving up a bed and bathroom back home. But if she can run the way she does living in a camper, with the money that's coming for the team from **Ortolan**, it could be a different world for her.

75   **NOEL**   Tea?

   LACES   No, haven't finished.

   NOEL   *(pours some tea)* Wish I'd got it together the way you have.

     Laces runs off.
     Enter Muriel and Pauline.

80   **MURIEL**   It wasn't your fault.

   PAULINE   It was.

   MURIEL   The stupid idiot was in the wrong lane.

   LACES   *(shouting to them)* Don't you dare try anything on that ankle until Dr Blackwood's seen it.

85   **MURIEL**   *(shouting)* I know.
     The thing you mustn't do is panic. Slowing down's a fatal mistake. If you stall, switch off the engine and start again.

   PAULINE   I'll never get the hang of it.

   MURIEL   You will.

90   *(Noel comes past them with Sue's things and some tea)*

     Morning.

   NOEL   Morning.

   PAULINE   You should park your camper up here. You could make a fortune from bacon sandwiches.

Ortolan   a fictional company that is sponsoring the women

| 95 | NOEL | Might end up doing that yet. *(He gestures to Sue)* Come on, get your things, have a shower. *(He goes with Sue)* |

Pauline and Muriel start to stretch and warm up.
Laces is doing press-ups. Enter Tom.

| | TOM | Morning. |

| 100 | PAULINE ⎱ MURIEL ⎰ | Morning |

| | TOM | Keep thinking I should get fit. Lose a bit of this. Had a girlfriend once, bought me a tracksuit. Think it was a hint. I find the mornings difficult. |

| | LACES | Can I help, Tom? |

| 105 | | *Tom gets down to look at Laces.* |

| | TOM | Laces Mackenzie? |

| | LACES | Yes. |

| | TOM | Used to be a great fan. |

| | LACES | Thanks. |

| 110 | TOM | They say you have a lot of trouble with your knee. |

| | LACES | Some days. |

| | | *Muriel is trying out her ankle.* |

| | TOM | Saw you run in Munich. One of the great moments of my life. Made one proud. Tears behind the eyes. Must |
| 115 | | help having something like that to remember. |

| | LACES | Yes. *(He shouts)* Farr, it'll be your own funeral. |

| | MURIEL | *(shouting back)* Spoil sport! |

| | TOM | Her injury bad? |

| | LACES | She's seeing the physio this morning. |

Kat and Zoe

Tony Jordan

This extract from an episode of *EastEnders* follows one of the series' best-known storylines. It shows that television acting – whilst different from stage acting – nevertheless demands a range of skills from actors. On occasions, two characters speak together for almost the whole episode; all the drama and tension are focused on them. Read the extract below, which involves many characters and moves swiftly between scenes and settings. (Kat has tried to commit suicide, after having revealed to her 'sister', Zoe, that Kat is, in fact, her mother). Then complete the activities on page 62.

Characters in order of appearance (5)

Lynne
Charlie
Mo
Little Mo
Harris (a doctor)

Scene 36/16. Hospital waiting room int. Night. 01.45. Studio D.

Charlie sits in waiting room. Lynne, Little Mo, Zoe and Mo enter.

LYNNE	Dad! Is she alright?	
CHARLIE	Still haven't heard.	
MO	We couldn't get a cab anywhere.	

5   **CHARLIE**   You're here now. *(Looks at Zoe)* You okay?

                     Zoe nods and sits down beside him.

      MO   Haven't they told you anything yet?

CHARLIE	No, they said they'd be out as soon as they knew anything.
10 LITTLE MO	She will be alright, won't she Dad?
CHARLIE	'Course she will.
LYNNE	We should never have left her on her own.
MO	We weren't to know she'd do something stupid.
LYNNE	Nan, this is Kat remember?

15 *Harris enters waiting room. Charlie sees her and stands.*

CHARLIE	Doctor ... How is she?
HARRIS	She's still poorly, but we've got things under control.

Visible relief from Charlie.

	As you know she had lacerations to both wrists. But 20 we've stitched her up and given her some fluids.
LYNNE	So she'll be alright?
HARRIS	She's stable now and is being taken up to intensive care. She's been drinking so we need to let her sleep it off and review her again in the morning.
25 CHARLIE	Thank God.
HARRIS	She'll also need to be seen by a psychiatrist.
CHARLIE	Why?
HARRIS	Your daughter slashed her wrists, I think she should talk to somebody.

30 *A beat, Charlie nods.*

I need to ask ... Are you sure she hasn't taken anything else?

MO	Like what?
HARRIS	Drugs?
35 **LITTLE MO**	Kat would never touch drugs.
CHARLIE	Is there a problem?
HARRIS	Well we haven't been able to rouse her but like I said it's almost certainly the amount of alcohol she's drunk. Don't worry; we'll keep an eye on her. The best thing you can do now is go home, call us in the morning.
40	
CHARLIE	Thank you doctor.

Harris smiles and walks away. Charlie sits back down.

LITTLE MO	We should call Belinda.
45 **LYNNE**	You are joking, the state she was in.
CHARLIE	Where is she?
LYNNE	We poured her in a cab, she's staying at a B&B in Hackney.
CHARLIE	We'll have to tell her.
50 **MO**	I'll do it.
LITTLE MO	She won't wanna come, you know what she's like about hospitals after Mum ...
CHARLIE	She doesn't have to, but she should know her sister's in here.
55 **MO**	I'll do it.
CHARLIE	Don't phone, go over there Mo, you got the address?
LYNNE	Yeah.

CHARLIE	That's if you can get in.
MO	I'll knock 'em up don't worry about that.

60   *Mo nods at Charlie, indicating she wants a word.*
      He joins her a few yards from others.

      What do I tell her?

CHARLIE	Eh?
MO	Belinda. Do I tell her everything or just that Kat's had

65   an accident?

      Charlie looks at others while he thinks.

CHARLIE	What d'you think?
MO	No sense in lying to her, not now.
CHARLIE	No.

70 | **MO** | There is another problem. |
| --- | --- |
| **CHARLIE** | What? |
| **MO** | *(Looks at Lynne)* That poor cow's supposed to be |

      getting married in the morning.

      Charlie reacts as he remembers.

75   You'd better see what she wants to do.

      Charlie nods. Mo walks away. Charlie gathers himself, then
      walks over to sit next to Lynne.

CHARLIE	Sweetheart ...

Activities

Spoonface Steinberg (page 32)

This powerful monologue places huge demands on the performer, even if it is 'only' performed as a radio play. And of course this is merely part of the play, which lasts almost an hour, and features only Spoonface's voice (and occasional music). In order to perform the piece, you need to read it carefully first, and do these activities.

Making

1. On a 'factual' level, what basic information do we learn about Spoonface? e.g. She's autistic.
2. Look at the first sentence. What do you notice about it? Why do you think Lee Hall chose to write Spoonface's speech in this way?
3. There is sadness – and humour – in what Spoonface tells us, and also in how she speaks. What is humorous? Find two or three examples. Is Spoonface aware she is funny?
4. Does Spoonface realise the exact nature of what is going on between her mother and father? Find evidence for what you think.

Performing and responding

Take part of the monologue – perhaps a page or part of a page – and try an initial read-aloud. Try to imitate how a child of this age might speak, but don't make your voice deliberately silly or high-pitched.

- Did Lee Hall's way of writing help you, or not?
- What did you find difficult?

You may already know some autistic children, but try to find out a little more about how they speak and behave – especially how they see others. If this was being performed as a stage play, how would Spoonface look? Would she be sitting? Standing? Moving around?

Try recording your section of monologue and listen to it. Have you found the right 'voice' for Spoonface?

Billy Liar (page 36)

Although this is quite a short monologue, and is part of the action of a play with many characters, it presents many of the problems any monologue has: how to keep the audience interested, and manage at the same time to tell us things about the person speaking.

Billy Liar is a play about a young man with three or four voices:

- his *entertaining* voice – the voice for amusing other people by making things up for a joke
- his *personal fantasy* voice – the voice he uses when he enters his own dreamworld
- his *I'm completely innocent!* voice for trying to get himself out of sticky situations.

Making

1. Go through the monologue on pages 36–37 and decide which voice to use for each section. Look in particular at the way he speaks to Duxbury in real life, and in his imagination.

2. When you have decided, think about the different vocal tones to use for each voice. Should the 'innocent' voice be hesitant and full of 'errs' and 'umms', as if Billy is making up his excuse on the spot?

Performing

Perform the speech aloud to a partner, or the rest of the group. Can your audience easily distinguish between Billy's three voices? If not, what do you need to do to make the three voices more different and distinctive?

Responding

Write your own short monologue in which you are answering the phone to a teacher who wants to know why you haven't come to school. Your best mate is with you, in the other room, also playing truant. Use three voices:

1. *'I'm innocent'* Err, sir, I'm sorry, but next door's dog bit me ...
2. *'fantasy'* Look, Mr Wood – I don't really have time for school with my United debut coming up ...
3. *'entertaining'* I've been tracking down Steve, who's here with me ...

Alibi (page 38)

Making

1. Read the play/monologue carefully, and then answer these questions:

- Who is Stephen waiting for?
- What made him try to make contact?
- What attitude does he have towards this person?

Having answered these questions, you should think about how to play the part of Stephen. Look carefully at any clues to his behaviour and way of speaking given in the stage directions. Think about the things Stephen says, too, and how he phrases his words.

2. Copy and complete the table below.

Example	Suggests?
Crosses his arms	Defiant? Defensive? Nervous?
He sighs	
'Happy now are you?'	
'I'm in charge now. Not used to that.'	
'You can hear my story.'	

3. Now take a small part of the monologue and work on individual words and phrases. Try out ways of saying the words, stressing some more than others, or saying some slowly, others in a rush. Example:

emphasise

This time *you* can do all the explaining.
Tell me your alibi for the *last   fourteen   years*.

stretch out words to make it seem a long time

Performing

Having done this, you should be able to reach some conclusions about Stephen's way of behaving. Remember, this whole monologue is performed to the audience, but as if the audience was the person he is waiting for.

Responding

Write a short commentary based on the work you have done, saying how you would advise someone to play the part of Stephen. Be very specific in your advice, suggesting how to say certain words or lines, how to move, etc.

How Crazy Are Those Who Love You So Much (page 42)

Making

Working in pairs, develop a dramatised performance of this poem, using your two voices to match the two voices in the poem.

First, decide how you will be positioned on stage as you perform. Consider several possibilities and make notes if you need to. For example ...

IDEA	MEANING?
Poet on chair, her lover/ husband standing behind	He has her imprisoned, his words of love are in fact the words of an interrogator
Poet standing on one side of room; her husband on the other. Both still	A wall between them. Coldness. Isolation. The words of love are meaningless throughout
Poet on chair; husband/ lover roaming the room, showing off what he has bought her	Her disgust/boredom with him; unimpressed with what he has to offer
A mix of all these used at different points in the poem	????

Try this out with a third person reading the poem, whilst you and your partner move as you have decided.

Performing

Try to learn the poem and then perform it as you have decided. Show it to other pairs who have also developed their own ideas.

Responding

Write an analysis of how you performed your version and what you intended to show. Did the audience get the impression you intended? How was your version different from others?

Try a new performance. This time, introduce at least one moment of contact between the two (if you didn't have any the first time). For example, try one or more of the following:

- a hand on the shoulder
- a hand clutching the wrist
- a stroke of the hair
- a hand under the chin, tilting the head up
- standing back to back, shoulders touching.

How does the chosen gesture (or gestures) change the meaning and effect?

Fear no more (page 43)

This is an *ironic* chant/song insofar as the young woman whom Guiderius and Arviragus believe to be dead is in fact their sister, and is not dead. However, this does not take away much from the power of the words. They believe her to be dead, so their sentiments are real.

But how do you deliver a funeral oration on stage? In the Royal Shakespeare Company's 2003 production of *Cymbeline* the two brothers were wild hunters, smeared with blood and earth. They chanted these words and beat their chests.

Making

Read the extract on pages 43–44 through several times, aloud, so that you feel comfortable with it. Now try two ways of performing this oration. First, say the words like a gentle prayer. Next, perform it as chant. You need not do the whole text to start with.

In both cases, make sure you understand the meaning of the words or the general feeling behind the words (e.g. soothing?).

Performing

The play is set in pre-Roman Britain, and there is a good deal of ritual (actions to do with ancient customs, offerings to gods, etc.). What movements might the two brothers perform before, during and after the funeral chant? Consider:

- flowers, herbs or other plants
- paint
- signals or gestures
- ways of arranging their 'dead' friend's body/hands, etc.

Try out some or all of these during your performance.

Responding

Find out more about the play *Cymbeline*. Why don't the brothers recognise their own sister? If she is the daughter of a king, why are they poor hunters?

Why is she drugged, and not dead? Why is she disguised?

Golden Girls (page 45)

There is a lot going on this script – different styles of speaking, different relationships, and lots of entrances and exits. Making sense of this can be difficult.

Making

1. Sue's long speech is almost poetic. Why is this? What does she talk about?

2. How do the next six or seven lines contrast with this speech?

Performing

Sue has just finished running when she gives her speech. Try to say her lines:

- standing still, hands on hips, breathing deeply (in control)
- hands on knees, bent double, panting (out of breath).

Which works best?

Responding

Each of the characters in this extract wants different things (and possibly the same things as well).

Sue's father Noel   wants Sue to push herself, to have a chance of benefiting from the best facilities on offer (e.g. sponsorship).

What does Sue want?   Look at what she says – does she want to succeed? Does she want to run? Does she want to impress her dad, or herself?

Look carefully at the text for clues into Sue's character and behaviour. Then write a short analysis of how Sue should be played in this scene. Tired? Fed up? Determined? Be very specific about her actions and gestures.

Kat and Zoe (page 50)

Making

Prepare a performance of this scene with a group. You will need at least five actors. Before you act it out, do a sit-down read-through, and get someone in your group to read the non-spoken sections (the pauses, changes of shot, character directions, etc.).

Now set your scene with three or four chairs, as if in a hospital waiting area.

The challenge you will face in performing this as a staged drama is that there is no camera to focus on individual characters. People will be seen even if they are not speaking.

So, decide ... how will Mo stand when Charlie is speaking to the doctor (Harris)?

How can you (as a group) direct the audience's attention towards Charlie and the doctor? For example, Mo and Little Mo must be focused on what Charlie, Lynne and Harris are saying.

Performing

Try out the scene in a number of ways, paying particular attention to how people stand, and how they look at each other. Then spend time on the way the lines are delivered.

Each person should think carefully about how to speak. Is there any humour in this extract? Who is in charge and making decisions? How will this affect the way he or she speaks?

When you perform the scene, try to perform it as if the script is new, and you had never seen these characters on screen. In other words, don't try to imitate the 'real' characters' voices – perform it in your own way.

Responding

Scripts, especially television soaps, often feature quite a few abbreviated sentences (*'Course she will*). Can you find any other examples of such sentences/lines in this script?

Development and extension

Monologues

A monologue is a speech given by one person, usually alone – although in some plays, one character speaks to the audience for a long time, while the other actors remain on stage.

1. Look back at the two monologues: *Spoonface Steinberg* and *Alibi*. On the surface they have little in common: one is spoken by a teenage boy; the other by a young girl. But there are similarities. Copy and complete this table.

Similarity	Spoonface	Stephen
Both have problems		*Parents abandoned him*
Both are outsiders	*Autism makes her different*	
Both have fathers who leave		*Left when Stephen was a baby*
Both are strong in their own ways		

2. Now create your own 'outsider' character. There are some suggestions below.

- someone new in an office
- a once-rich family with a single child moving to a large estate
- a newly-signed player in a football team, disliked by the others (perhaps he earns more than they do).

In pairs, improvise a conversation where an 'outsider' tells another person about their life. The listener does not have a character – he or she can only agree, or ask simple questions, e.g: *How did that happen? How did you feel? What happened next? I see. I understand,* etc.

Once you have developed a character, write out your monologue as a script of about two pages. Look back at *Alibi* and *Spoonface Steinberg* for ideas on how to set it out, how to build in pauses, and how to keep it interesting.

- What tense will you write it in?
- How will you use pauses and simple movements?
- What story will you tell? Will there be a key incident or moment?

Ritual

Ceremonies – whether they are in modern settings (birthday parties, weddings, church services, funerals, awards functions, etc.) or older ones (sacrifices, oaths of allegiance, etc.) – have at their heart certain rituals. These might be to do with the order of events, special objects, agreed forms of words, etc.

In pairs, make a list of the ritualistic elements that make up a marriage, e.g. cutting the wedding cake; the speeches, etc. Then choose one of the titles below and invent your own ritualised performance based on an ancient ceremony.

- *The sacrifice*
- *Choosing the next king*
- *Oath of allegiance*
- *Harvest ceremony.*

As part of the performance, include some or all of the following:

- ordered and sequenced movement (e.g. a procession or a dance)
- chants, songs or poems
- a clear sense of the start and end of the ceremony
- appropriate ritualised language (appeal to the gods? powerful words?)

As part of this preparation, think carefully about how you will *frame* each scene. Drama can be seen as a series of photos or pictures that are especially appropriate for ceremony or ritual. Each framed moment can take into account:

- how people stand in relation to each other (backs turned? arms folded?)
- where people are looking (away from someone? directly at them?)
- levels (is everyone at the same height, or are some lower/higher?)

This should lead you to a judgement about *where* you are directing the audience's attention (which will be intimately connected with your decisions about how each scene is framed).

Chapter 3: Scriptings

Play scripts can take many styles and forms. This chapter gives you the opportunity to explore a wide range of them. It looks at how writers create characters and settings; how staging and movement add to dramatic effect; and how a writer uses different types of speech. Because monologues, and works by Shakespeare, are covered elsewhere in *Page to Stage*, these do not appear in this section.

In this chapter you will:
- explore how writers capture an audience's attention through empathy, humour, shock, dramatic irony, etc.
- look at the characterisation of people in scripts
- learn about the staging and setting of plays
- study how writers explore the same themes in different ways.

Ernie's Incredible Illucinations

Alan Ayckbourn

Alan Ayckbourn is one of Britain's best-loved dramatists; his plays are performed in theatres all over the country. Most of his work has a comic or absurd side to it, and often involves character mix-ups and elements of farce, though sometimes with a serious side. This extract from one of his earlier plays involves a boy called Ernie, who has been having daydreams. His anxious parents take him to the doctor, who asks them when the 'illucinations' (a cross between 'hallucinations' and 'illusions') started. Read through the extract then complete the activities on page 102.

Characters in order of appearance (5)

Doctor
Mum
Dad
Ernie
Officer

	DOCTOR	Perhaps it would be better if you told me a little more about it. When did you first notice this …?

DOCTOR Perhaps it would be better if you told me a little more about it. When did you first notice this …?

MUM Ah well …

DAD Ah.

5 MUM Now then …

DAD Now …

MUM He'd have been … well, it'd have been about … near enough … er …

DOCTOR Go on.

10 *Ernie steps forward. During his speech Mum and Dad remain seated. The Doctor moves to the side of the stage, produces a notebook and makes notes on what follows.*

ERNIE	It started with these daydreams. You know, the sort everybody gets. Where you suddenly score a hat trick in the last five minutes of the Cup Final or you bowl out the West Indies for ten runs … or saving your granny from a blazing helicopter, all that sort of rubbish.
	It was one wet Saturday afternoon and me and my Mum and my Dad were all sitting about in the happy home having one of those exciting afternoon rave-ups we usually have in our house.
	Ernie sits at the table in the doctor's chair and starts to read a book. Mum has started knitting and Dad just sits, gazing ahead of him. A long silence.
ERNIE	It was all go in our house.
	Pause.
MUM	I thought you'd be at the match today, Albert.
DAD	Not today.
MUM	Not often you miss a game.
DAD	They're playing away.
MUM	Oh.
DAD	In Birmingham. I'm blowed if I'm going to Birmingham. Even for United.
ERNIE	Meanwhile … while this exciting discussion was in progress, I was reading this book about the French wartime resistance workers and of the dangers they faced … often arrested in their homes. I started wondering what would happen if a squad of soldiers turned up at our front door, having been tipped off about the secret radio transmitter hidden in our cistern … when suddenly …

The tramp of feet, and a squad of soldiers comes marching on and up to their front door.

OFFICER   Halte! *(He bangs on the door)*

45   *Pause.*

DAD   That the door?

MUM   What?

DAD   The door.

MUM   Was it?

50   OFFICER   Open zis door. Open the door! *(He knocks again)*

MUM   Oh, that'll be the milkman wanting his money. He always comes round about now. Albert, have you got ten bob?

DAD   *(fumbling in his pockets)* Ah …

OFFICER   *(shouting)* Open zis door immediately. Or I shall order
55   my men to break it down. *(He bangs on the door again)*

MUM   Just a minute. Coming.

DAD   Should have one somewhere …

OFFICER   We know you're in there, English spy! Come out with your hands up …

60   MUM   What's he shouting about? Oh, I'd better ask him for three pints next week, if Auntie May's coming …

OFFICER   Zis is your last chance … *(He knocks again)*

MUM   Oh shut up …

  The Officer signals his men. Two of them step back, brace
65   *their shoulders and prepare to charge the door.*

MUM   I'm coming … I'm coming.

	ERNIE	I shouldn't go out there, Mum …
	MUM	What?
	ERNIE	I said don't go out there …
70	MUM	What?
	ERNIE	It's not the milkman. It's a squad of enemy soldiers …
	MUM	Who?
	ERNIE	They've come for me …
	MUM	Who has?
75	ERNIE	The soldiers. They've found out about the radio transmitter …
	MUM	What radio?
	DAD	Hey, here, that's a point. Have you paid our telly licence yet, Ethel? It might be the detector van.
80	MUM	Oh, sit down, Albert. Stop worrying. It's just Ernie. Shut up, Ernie.
	ERNIE	But Mum …
	DAD	I think I'll take the telly upstairs. Just in case …

The soldiers charge at the door. A loud crash.

85	ERNIE	Don't go out, Mum.
	MUM	Shut up.
	DAD	*(struggling with the set)* Just take it upstairs.
	ERNIE	Don't go.
90	MUM	I can't leave him out there. The way he's going he'll have the door off its hinges in a minute … *(She moves to the door)*

| DAD | Mind your backs. Out of my way … |

| ERNIE | Mum … |

95 | | *Mum opens the door just as the two soldiers are charging for the second time. They shoot past her, straight into the hall, collide with Dad and land in a heap with him. Dad manages to hold the TV set above his head and save it from breaking.* |

| MUM | Hey … |

| DAD | Oy! |

100 | | *The Officer and the other soldiers enter. Ernie crouches behind the table.* |

| OFFICER | Ah-ha! The house is surrounded. |

| MUM | Who are you ? |

| OFFICER | Put up your hands. My men will search the house. |

105 | DAD | *(feebly)* Hey … |

| OFFICER | *(shouting up the stairs)* We know you're hiding in here, you can't get away … |

| DAD | Hey … *hey* … HEY! |

| OFFICER | Ah-ha. What have we here? |

110 | DAD | Oh. It's the telly. The neighbour's telly. Not mine. |

| OFFICER | Ah-ha. |

| DAD | Just fixing it for him, you see … |

| OFFICER | Outside. |

| DAD | Eh? |

115 | OFFICER | You will come with me. |

| DAD | What, in this? I'm not going out in this rain. |

OFFICER	Outside or I shoot.
DAD	Here …
MUM	Albert …
120 ERNIE	Hold it. Drop those guns.
OFFICER	Ah, so … *(He raises his gun)*
ERNIE	Da-da-da-da-da-da-da-da-da-da-da.

The soldiers collapse and are strewn all over the hall. Mum screams. Then a silence.

125 MUM	Oh, Ernie. What have you done?
ERNIE	Sorry, Mum.
DAD	Oh, lad …
MUM	Are they – dead?
DAD	Yes.
130	*(Mum screams again)*
DAD	Steady, steady. This needs thinking about.
MUM	What about the neighbours?
DAD	Could create a bit of gossip, this could.

Eclipse

Simon Armitage

This is an extract from a short play by the poet Simon Armitage. It describes events surrounding the total eclipse of the sun in 1999. The play takes place in Cornwall, and focuses on a group of young people, including Midnight, a boy who is blind, and a firm believer in God. Lucy, a girl who has come down with her parents to see the eclipse, joins the group, and bets them she can make Midnight tell a lie. Read through the extract then complete the activities on pages 103–104.

Characters in order of appearance (7)

Lucy
Midnight
Tulip
Glue Boy
Polly
Jane
Klondike

Lucy and Glue Boy approach Midnight. Lucy taps him on the shoulder.

	LUCY	Listen.
	MIDNIGHT	What?
	LUCY	Can you hear a boat?
5	MIDNIGHT	Nope.
	LUCY	Listen, I can hear its engine. I'm certain.
	MIDNIGHT	I think you're mistaken.
	LUCY	There, just as I thought, coming round the point.
	MIDNIGHT	There can't be. Which direction?
10	TULIP	*(to the others)* What's she saying, there's no boat.

LUCY	Straight out in front. Plain as the nose on your face. See it, Glue Boy?
GLUE BOY	Er ... ? Oh, sure.
LUCY	It's a trawler. Is it greeny-blue, would you say?
15 **GLUE BOY**	Well, sort of sea-green, sort of sky-blue, sort of blue moon sort of colour.
LUCY	I'm amazed you can't hear it, it's making a real racket.
MIDNIGHT	Well, I ...
LUCY	Too much time with the ear-plugs, listening to static.
20 **MIDNIGHT**	My hearing's perfect.
LUCY	Fine. OK. Forget it.
MIDNIGHT	I'm sorry, I didn't mean to be rude.
LUCY	You weren't. I shouldn't have mentioned it. It's my fault – I should have thought. You can't hear the boat for the sound of the sea-gulls.
25	
MIDNIGHT	Sea-gulls?
POLLY	*(to the others)* There isn't a bird for miles.
JANE	This is a waste of time. It's her who's telling the lies.
LUCY	All that high-pitched skriking and screaming. Must play havoc with sensitive hearing, like yours.
30	
MIDNIGHT	How close?
LUCY	The birds? Three hundred yards, five hundred at most. Black-headed gulls, Glue Boy, don't you think?
GLUE BOY	Well, kind of rare breed, kind of less common, kind of lesser-spotted type things.
35	
LUCY	Don't say you're going deaf?

MIDNIGHT	Who, me?
LUCY	Glue Boy can hear them, and he's out of his head. Come on, Midnight, stop clowning around. I bet you can hear it all. I bet you can hear a cat licking its lips in the next town, can't you?
MIDNIGHT	I don't know ... I think sometimes I filter it out.
LUCY	Yes, when you're half asleep. But listen, what can you hear now?
MIDNIGHT	Er ... something ...
LUCY	That aeroplane for a start, I bet.
MIDNIGHT	Yes. The aeroplane.
LUCY	I can't see it myself, where would you say it was?
MIDNIGHT	Er ... off to the left, that's my guess.
LUCY	What else? That dog on the cliff, half a mile back. Can you hear that?
MIDNIGHT	Yes. The dog. Sniffing the air is it? Scratching the ground?
LUCY	Amazing. Wrap-around-sound. What else? The boy with the kite?
MIDNIGHT	Yes, the kite. The wind playing the twine like a harp. It's a wonderful sound.
LUCY	And Klondike and Tulip, coming back up the beach. What are they talking about?
MIDNIGHT	They're saying ... this and that, about the eclipse, and how dark and how strange it'll be.
LUCY	And down by the rock pools, the twins?

MIDNIGHT	Chatting away. Girls' things. Boyfriends, that kind of
65	stuff. It's not really fair to listen in on it.
LUCY	You're not kidding. You're absolutely ultra-sonic. Glue Boy, how about that for a pair of ears?
GLUE BOY	Yeah, he's **Jodrell Bank**, he is.
LUCY	And one last noise. A siren or something?
70 MIDNIGHT	Car alarm.
LUCY	No. Music.
MIDNIGHT	Brass band. Floral Dance.
LUCY	No. It's there on the tip of my tongue but I just can't place it. You know, sells lollies and things.
75 MIDNIGHT	Ice-cream van. Ice-cream van. I can hear it.
LUCY	You can?
MIDNIGHT	Can't you?
LUCY	No. Not any more. What was the tune?
MIDNIGHT	Er ... Greensleeves.
80 LUCY	Greensleeves eh? Thanks, Midnight, that should do it.
MIDNIGHT	Sorry?
TULIP	Nice one, stupid.
MIDNIGHT	What? I thought you were ...
TULIP	Yeah, well, you know what thought did.
85 POLLY	Pathetic, Midnight.
JANE	You should see a doctor, you're hearing voices.

Jodrell Bank   an observatory with a large radio telescope

MIDNIGHT   But, all those noises ...

KLONDIKE   She made them up...

Lost on the streets

Michele Celeste

These scenes come from the play *Mariza's Story*. They describe the experiences of Mariza, a young girl from a poor family, on the streets of a South American city. Mariza, who is eight years old, has become lost, and is searching for her sister Tania, and her mother. Read through the extract then complete the activities on page 105.

Characters in order of appearance (3)

Marcelo
Mariza
Mariza's Mother (doesn't speak)
Old Woman

Scene Eight

Day. The city. Mariza comes on and walks through the city. By now completely lost, she picks up rubbish from a bin to eat. She finds an unfinished can of Coke from the bin and drinks from it. Then, behind Mariza, a discarded fridge cardboard box takes on life. It stealthily moves
5 *towards her with unfriendly intentions. At the last moment, Mariza hears it and turns. She screams and backs away. The box corners her.*

Mariza, as a last resort, holds out her can of drink. A hand comes out of the box and grabs it. Noisy drinking from inside. The can is tossed out. Marcelo, inside the box, speaks in a strange voice.

10   **MARCELO**   I'm sorry. I didn't realise you were thirsty.

                    He speaks accusingly.

                    Another runaway! Oh-oh!

                    Mariza is scared.

                    What are you doing in a big city like this?

15	MARIZA	I ... I ... I'm looking for my mum.
	MARCELO	Looking for your mum, eh?
	MARIZA	And my sister, Tania.
	MARCELO	I have heard all sorts of excuses from you lot.
	MARIZA	It's true!
20	MARCELO	Where do you think you'll find your mum and sister then?

Mariza shrugs. There is a pause.

Where!

	MARIZA	I ... I don't know.
25	MARCELO	You're a runaway!
	MARIZA	No ... I'm not a runaway.
	MARCELO	Have you seen how many children are living on the streets here?
	MARIZA	I ... I've just got here.
30	MARCELO	Ah-ha! The street is no place for a little girl.
	MARIZA	I'm only looking for ...

Marcelo cuts in.

	MARCELO	Be warned! If a cop nicks you, he'll send you into an orphanage, where they beat you all the time! Aren't you scared now?
35		

Mariza nods. There is a pause.

Why don't you go back home?

	MARIZA	Home? Which way's my home?

MARCELO	Oh, yes, go on pretending you're lost. Dirty clothes, broken shoes. There you are. Good advice is lost on urchins like you.

The box makes an attempt to grab Mariza.

MARIZA	Aaaahhhhh!

Mariza drops her coat and runs off. Marcelo, a street kid, comes out of the box and laughs.

MARCELO	Ha! Ha! Ha! What do I see there? Another kid, newcomer to the city. Ha! Ha! Ha! I'll give him a fright too. Ha! Ha! Ha!

He gets back into the box and exits laughing.

Scene Nine

Mum looking for Mariza in the city. She finds Mariza's coat on the ground and picks it up. With renewed hope, she exits looking for her daughters.

Scene Ten

Night. A shocked and very tired Mariza comes on, scared of all those immense buildings and not a human being in sight. She stumbles into someone sleeping on the pavement, totally enveloped in a blanket on a cardboard sheet. She rushes away scared. But the sleeper has not moved. Not seeing any other human being around, hesitantly, she goes back and peeps under the blanket trying to see the face of the sleeper, believing to have caught a glimpse of her mum.

MARIZA	Mum? Mum?
OLD WOMAN	What?
MARIZA	Are you my mum?

An Old Woman who lives on the streets, emerges from the blanket, and mutters to herself.

OLD WOMAN	Waking me up in the middle of the night.
65 **MARIZA**	Are you my mum?
OLD WOMAN	Your mum!? I never had a child in my life! I'm not like some who call themselves mothers and then abandon their children on the street!
MARIZA	You are too old.
70 **OLD WOMAN**	You bet I am! I'm too old.
MARIZA	When I first saw you, I thought you were my mum.
OLD WOMAN	I'm not your mum!
MARIZA	I saw you sleeping like my mum.
OLD WOMAN	Oh.
75 **MARIZA**	Can you help me?
OLD WOMAN	How can I help you?
MARIZA	To find my mum?
OLD WOMAN	Where do you come from?
MARIZA	I come from?
80 **OLD WOMAN**	Can't you remember?
MARIZA	Brazil.
OLD WOMAN	Brazil? That's a large place.
MARIZA	You know where it is?
OLD WOMAN	We are in Brazil! Everywhere you go in this country
85	is Brazil!
MARIZA	Where can I find my mum, then?
OLD WOMAN	Brazil is a country! Like, like, ehm, like ...

(She is at a loss)

Ah! Like Spain! Portugal. England. It's a large place. Now you must tell me the place where your mum lives, the town, the street name and the number of the house.

MARIZA   I think I come from ... Medina?

OLD WOMAN   I don't know where is this Mellina.

MARIZA   Not Mellina. Me ... rina!

OLD WOMAN   Marina?

MARIZA   Not Marina. Mellina!

OLD WOMAN   Oh, Medina!

MARIZA   Marina!

OLD WOMAN   Messina!

MARIZA   Messiah!

OLD WOMAN   Messiah?!

They are both totally confused.

MARIZA   It is what I said the first time. Now I don't remember anymore.

OLD WOMAN   Ask a policeman.

MARIZA   If a policeman finds me, he'll send me to a orphanage!

OLD WOMAN   Write the name then, where you come from on the cardboard.

Mariza takes a felt pen and tries, but as she cannot write, draws a woman without a head.

What does it say?

MARIZA	This is my mum.
115 OLD WOMAN	Oh, I can't see very well.
MARIZA	I only went a year to school.
OLD WOMAN	I never went to school at all. So, this is your mum's name?
MARIZA	Yes.
120 OLD WOMAN	Oh, I see. Looks like a drawing to me. My eyes. Well, I'm sorry I don't know. You woke me up in the middle of my sleep! I can't sleep well and you woke me up when I was sleeping so well … dreaming.

The Old Woman prepares to sleep again. Mariza, who is
125 *very tired, starts to go. But where? She stops and goes*
back.

MARIZA	Can I sleep here?
OLD WOMAN	Sleep here?
MARIZA	I'm very tired.
130 OLD WOMAN	Do what you like. Just don't wake me up.

The Old Woman goes to sleep. Mariza sleeps by her.

Sparkleshark

Philip Ridley

The writer Philip Ridley is as well known for his children's novels as for his plays, and this extract from one of his plays has much in common with his fiction – notably the same love of vivid and inventive language.

This is the opening part of a play set in the East End of London. Jake has gone up on the roof of a tower block to continue his writing, and to keep out of the way of certain people from school. Read through the extract then complete the activities on pages 106–107.

Characters in order of appearance (3)

Jake
Polly
Finn

The rooftop of a tower block in the East End of London. Many TV aerials and satellite dishes, a large puddle, discarded household furniture, piles of rubbish and various scattered detritus.

Some metal steps lead from the main larger area of roof up to a tiny
5 *platform. There's a doorway here, leading to the emergency stairs. This is the only entrance to the roof.*

It is about 4.30 in the afternoon. Mid-September. The weather is sunny.

Jake enters. He is fourteen years old, slightly built and clutching a satchel. He is wearing a well-worn, but still clean and tidy, school uniform
10 *and glasses (the left lens is cracked and the bridge held together by sticky tape). His hair is neatly cut.*

Jake makes his way down to main area of roof and sits in an old armchair. He is familiar and comfortable with these surroundings. It's a place he's been many times before – his secret hideaway.

15 *Jake takes notebook from satchel and reads, nodding and murmuring thoughtfully. Then he takes a pen from inside pocket and writes.*

JAKE	Big … fish! Bigfish! … No, no.

Tears page from notebook, screws it up and throws it aside. Starts pacing the roof and continues to write –

20 Glitter! Glitterpiranha! … No, no.

Polly enters. She is fourteen years old and wearing the same school uniform as Jake, although hers is brand new (and has a skirt instead of trousers). Her hair is longish, but held primly in place by an elastic band. She is clutching a tiny tool box.

25 *Polly watches Jake from the raised platform.*

JAKE	Shark! Yes! Shark … glitter –

Jake turns and sees Polly. He lets out a yelp of surprise and drops his notebook. Loose pages flutter everywhere.

POLLY	Oh, I'm sorry.

30 *Jake starts picking up pages. Polly climbs down metal steps and starts helping him.*

JAKE	Don't bother.
POLLY	No bother.

(Picks page from puddle)

35 This one's a bit soggy. Can't quite read –

JAKE	*(snatching it from her)* Don't! This is … it's personal stuff. You can't just stroll up here and start reading things willy-nilly! Watch out! You're treading on one now! You should be in a circus with feet that size. What you doing here
40 | | anyway! This is *my* place! Go away! |

Pause.

POLLY	I've only got three things to say to you. One: what I'm doing up here is none of your business. Two: the roof is

---

not your private property – unless, of course, you have a special clause in your rent book, which I doubt. And three: I find it strange that someone who can write such magical words has such a spiteful tongue in his head … Now, I've got something I need to do, then I'll be gone. In the interim, I'd be grateful if you didn't speak to me again.

Goes to satellite dish that's positioned on the edge of the roof. She opens tool box, removes screwdriver and – none too convincingly – starts fiddling. Pause.

JAKE   Is it really magical?

POLLY   … What?

JAKE   My writing.

POLLY   Bits.

Pause.

JAKE   I … I was wondering whose dish that was.

Pause.

I'm Jake.

POLLY   I know.

JAKE   How?

POLLY   Oh, please – Your eyes! Use them! *(Indicates her school uniform)*

JAKE   You go to my school!

POLLY   Started last week.

JAKE   Haven't seen you.

POLLY   Not surprised. All you do is hide between those two big dustbins at the back of the playground.

70	JAKE	I like it there.
	POLLY	But, surely, they're a bit … well, smelly?
	JAKE	Don't notice after a few deep breaths.
	FINN	*(offstage)* AAARGHHNAAAHHH!

Polly leans over ledge.

75	POLLY	All right, Finn! Tell me when it gets better.
	FINN	*(offstage)* AAARGHHNAAAHH!

Polly continues fiddling with satellite dish.

	JAKE	That … that voice! I've seen it – I mean, I've seen who it belongs to. He joined my class last week.
80	POLLY	That's my baby brother.
	JAKE	Baby! But … but he's huge! He grabbed two desks. One in each hand. And lifted them up. Above his head.
	POLLY	I suppose even you would have to notice that.
85	JAKE	The teachers want him expelled already. All the boys are scared of him. They call him the Monster –
	POLLY	He's not a monster! Everyone calls him that! Everywhere he goes! But he's not! He's very gentle! Cries easily, if you must know.
	FINN	*(offstage)* AARGHHNAAAH!
90	POLLY	*(calling)* OK, Finn! *(at Jake)* It's getting better.
	JAKE	You understand him?
	POLLY	It might sound like a meaningless groan to you but – believe me – once you grasp the nuances, it's a very subtle form of communication.

| 95 | **FINN** | *(offstage)* AARRGHHNAAAHHH! |

| | **JAKE** | Subtle? That? |

| | **POLLY** | Well, he's in a bad mood. Missing his favourite programme. The one with real-life accidents. You know? Housewives setting themselves on fire with dodgy hairdryers – |

100

| | **FINN** | *(offstage)* AAAH! |

| | **POLLY** | All right, Finn! – And everyone watches these programmes because they're supposed to be educational – |

| | **JAKE** | But all they really want to see is someone's head getting sliced off by helicopter blades. |

105

| | **POLLY** | Precisely. |

| | **FINN** | *(offstage)* AAAH! |

| | **POLLY** | Thanks, Finn! – That's it! He'll quieten now. Picture's perfect. Well, perfect as it'll ever be with this equipment. |

110

Starts packing up tools etc.

Dad got it cheap somewhere. I'm sure there's bits missing. And there was no instruction manual. Haven't a clue what I'm doing really – You know anything about this sort of thing?

115 **JAKE** All I know for sure is you've got to aim the dish at a satellite up there.

POLLY Perhaps I should put it higher – Oh!

JAKE What?

POLLY A dead bird … Poor thing. Only a baby. Must have fallen
120 from one of the nests.

Peers closer at dead bird.

All mauve and scarlet. Little yellow beak. Come and have a look.

JAKE   Rather not.

125 POLLY   Can't hurt you.

JAKE   Not that … I can be seen up there. By people in the football pitch.

POLLY   But there's no one in the football pitch.

JAKE   But there might be. Any minute now. If he sees me – oh,
130   you won't understand.

POLLY   Try me.

My Mother Said I Never Should

Charlotte Keatley

Like the previous piece, this is the opening to a play. The play shows four women at various times in their lives over the course of fifty years or so, appearing both as adults and – here – as children. What is unusual is that the four are related: Doris (the great grandmother); Margaret (the grandmother), Jackie (the mother) and Rosie (the daughter). The play is not naturalistic, then, and their meeting is one that could never have actually taken place. Read through the extract then complete the activities on pages 108–109.

Characters in order of appearance (4)

Rosie (aged 8)
Doris (aged 5)
Margaret (aged 9)
Jackie (aged 9)

Scene One

The Wasteground, a place where girls come to play.

Enter four girls, each dressed contemporary to her own generation, singing:

My Mother said I never should,
5   Play with the gypsies in the wood,
If I did, she would say,
Naughty girl to disobey!

ROSIE   *(chanting)* What are little girls made of? *(coaxing Doris to answer)* Ssh …

10 DORIS   Sugar – and – *(effort)* – spice … ?

MARGARET   And …

DORIS   *(hesitantly)* And?

MARGARET	All Things Nice.

Doris squirming, doesn' t want to repeat it.

	JACKIE	*(can' t bear it any longer)* Let's kill our Mummy.
15	MARGARET	Whose Mummy?
	DORIS	Whose Mam? *(copying)*
	ROSIE	Yes, whose Mum?
	JACKIE	All our Mummies if you like?
20	ROSIE	Who's going to do it?
	MARGARET	*(to Jackie)* Dare you!
	DORIS	… Dare you …
	JACKIE	We'll all do it.
	MARGARET	It's my teatime …
25	ROSIE	How?
	JACKIE	I dunno … Boiling oil.
	DORIS	… Dare you … *(repeating)*
	MARGARET	Shut up, baby.
	JACKIE	Tell you what –
30	ROSIE	What –
	JACKIE	I've got a penknife. I've been keeping it for something special.
	ROSIE	You pinched it off Jimmy Tucker!
	JACKIE	And we'll get some string, and take Mummy down by
35		the railway line where there's a hole in the fence, and I think you have to put a stake through her heart.

	ROSIE	We couldn't do them *all*. *(Pause)* We haven't got enough string.
40	JACKIE	Just ours, then. *(Conspiratorial)* They're not in our gang. Also they don't count because they're babies. They can do their own Mummys when they're old enough.
	MARGARET	Do mine! – I don't like blood …
	JACKIE	Lucy Parker cut her finger off at school.
	MARGARET	I'll be sick.
45	JACKIE	Only the top bit. *(Pause)* Like a flap.
	DORIS	… Flip flap flop …
	ROSIE	*(bends to Doris)* Do you want us to do your Mum?
	MARGARET	She's too young to know.
50	JACKIE	She's got no Daddy: if we do her Mummy, she'll be an orphan and then we'll be responsible.
	MARGARET	Her Mummy's all right — She gave us lemonade. *(Pause)*
	ROSIE	… She'll split on us though. Then we'll be outlaws.
	JACKIE	Go away, baby.
55		*(Doris cries)*
	JACKIE	Go on. Go home. *(Pushes Doris away)* Tea? Tea time.
	ALL	Tea time. Tea time.
		Doris goes.
	JACKIE	Piggy.
60	MARGARET	She'd only cry when she saw the blood. Me, I'm not having any babies.

ROSIE	How d'you know?
MARGARET	I'm not getting married.
ROSIE	*(pause. Thinks)* Well it still might grow.
65 MARGARET	What?
ROSIE	The seed. The baby seed, inside you.
MARGARET	It can't! Can it?

Jackie has been arranging sweet wrappers

ROSIE	What are you doing?
70 JACKIE	Voodoo. We need bits of her fingernail and hair and stuff.
ROSIE	… She might haunt us …
JACKIE	You don't know *anything,* do you.

Rosie is subdued. Margaret comes to look

75 MARGARET	What's that for?
ROSIE	Voodoo, you wally.
JACKIE	We're going to have a seance. To call up … spirits from beyond the grave.
MARGARET	We do that at school.
80 JACKIE	Do you?
MARGARET	On Fridays. Take buttercups apart, and count their … sta – stay – … bits.
JACKIE	Shh! Hold hands. *(They obey)* You have to repeat after me.
85 MARGARET ROSIE	} After me.

Lights dim a bit.

JACKIE   *(deepens voice)* We call up the spirit of – Granny!

JACKIE
MARGARET   } We call up the spirit of Granny!

JACKIE   Who died three years ago last Wednesday. And lived
90   in Twickenham. Amen.

MARGARET
ROSIE   } Amen.

Lights darken.

MARGARET   It's getting dark …

ROSIE   … What happens now? …

95   JACKIE   *(deep voice)* YOU from beyond the grave! Tell us how
to kill Mummy!

Lights almost blackout. Silence.

JACKIE   YOU from beyond the grave, tell us –

Margaret and Rosie see something, scream and run off.

100   *Figure of Doris now as Gran appears upstage, walking
slowly towards them.*

JACKIE   Mummy! Mummy! *(runs off after the others)*

*Doris continues to walk forward, oblivious of above. She
removes a dustsheet of World War Two blackout material
105   from a large object which it has been completely covering.
It is a baby grand piano. Margaret is crouching underneath
it, hidden from Doris by a pile of bedding also under the
piano. Doris begins to dust the piano as the lights rise for
Scene Two and the wireless begins to play.*

Blood Brothers

Willy Russell

This scene is taken from *Blood Brothers*, one of the longest-running stage shows in London. Written by Willy Russell, also famous for his plays *Educating Rita* and *Shirley Valentine*, it tells the story of two boys growing up in Liverpool. The boys are in fact brothers, separated at birth, though neither is aware of this fact and they have grown up with very different backgrounds. Read through the extract then complete the activities on pages 110–111.

Characters in order of appearance (4)

Eddie
Mickey
The Mother
Mrs Lyons

EDDIE		Will you be my best friend?
MICKEY		Yeh. Yeh if you want.
EDDIE		And I shall be your best friend. What's your name?
MICKEY	5	Michael Johnston. But everyone calls me Mickey. What's yours?
EDDIE		Edward.
MICKEY		And they call you Eddie?
EDDIE		No!
MICKEY		Well I will.
EDDIE	10	Will you?
MICKEY		Yeh. How old are you, Eddie?
EDDIE		Seven.
MICKEY		I'm older than you. I'm nearly eight.

EDDIE	Well I'm nearly eight really.
15 MICKEY	When's your birthday?
EDDIE	December the twelfth.
MICKEY	So is mine.
EDDIE	Is it really?
MICKEY	Hey, we were born on the same day. That means we can be blood brothers. Do you want to be my blood brother, Eddie?

20

EDDIE	What do I have to do?
MICKEY	It hurts you know. *(Mickey taking out his penknife, cuts his hand)* Now give us your hand. *(Does the same to Eddie and then clamps the hands together)* See this means that we're blood brothers and that we always have to stand by each other. Now, you have to say, after me: 'I will always defend my brother ... '

25

EDDIE	I will always defend my brother ...
30 THE MOTHER	*(Off)* Mickey ... Mickey ...
EDDIE	Is that your mummy?

(The Mother appearing)

MICKEY	Mam, this is my brother.
THE MOTHER	*(Stunned)* What?
35 MICKEY	My blood brother, Eddie.
THE MOTHER	Eddie. Eddie who?
EDDIE	Edward Lyons, Mrs Johnston.

(The Mother stares at him)

MICKEY	Eddie's my best friend now, Mam. He lives up by the park but ...

40

THE MOTHER	Mickey, get in the house …
MICKEY	What?
THE MOTHER	*(Threatening)* Get in!
	(The bright and eager smile disappears from Eddie's face)
45 MICKEY	But I've only ...
THE MOTHER	Get!
MICKEY	*(Going, almost crying)* I haven't done nothing. I'll see you, Eddie.
EDDIE	Erm. Erm have I done something, Mrs Johnston?
50 THE MOTHER	Does your mother know you're down here? *(Eddie shaking his head)* What would she say if she knew?
EDDIE	I … I think she'd be angry.
THE MOTHER	So don't you think you'd better go home before she finds out?
55 EDDIE	I suppose so.
THE MOTHER	Go on then.
	(He turns to go and then stops)
EDDIE	Could I ... would it be all right if I came to play with Mickey on another day? Or perhaps he could come 60 and play at my house ...
THE MOTHER	Don't you ever come around here again. Ever.
EDDIE	But …
THE MOTHER	Ever! Now go on ... beat it ... go on, go home before the bogey man gets you.
65	*(She watches as he leaves and stands, staring after him)*

Act 2, scene 3

She watches as the scene forms in which we see Eddie at home, leafing through a dictionary, Mrs Lyons entering and kissing him on the head.

EDDIE *(turning and smiling at her)* Mum ... Mummy ...

70 *(The Mother turns and leaves)*

EDDIE Mum how do you spell 'bogey man'?

MRS LYONS *(Laughing)* Wherever did you hear such a word'?

EDDIE I erm ... I'm trying to look it up ... what is a bogey man?

75 **MRS LYONS** *(Laughing)* Edward ... there's no such thing. It's erm, it's just an idea of something bad. It's a, a superstition. The sort of thing a silly mother would say to her children 'the bogey man will get you'.

EDDIE Will he get me?

80 **MRS LYONS** Edward ... I've told you, there's no such thing.

(There is a loud knocking at the door. Mrs Lyons goes off to answer the door)

MICKEY *(Off)* Does Eddie live here?

MRS LYONS Pardon?

85 **MICKEY** Does he? Is he coming out to play?

EDDIE *(Looking up. Delighted)* Mickey!

(Mrs Lyons and Mickey entering)

MICKEY Hiya, Eddie. Look, I've got our Sammy's catapult. You coming out eh?

90 **EDDIE** *(Taking the catapult and trying a practice shot)* Ogh ... Isn't Mickey fantastic, Mum?

MRS LYONS	Do you go to the same school as Edward?
MICKEY	No.
EDDIE	Mickey says smashing things. We're blood brothers, aren't we, Mickey?
MICKEY	Yeh. We were born on the same day.
EDDIE	Come on Mickey ... Let's go ...!
MRS LYONS	Edward! Edward it's time for bed.
EDDIE	Mummy, it's not.
MRS LYONS	*(Ushering Mickey out)* I'm very sorry but it's Edward's bedtime.
EDDIE	Mummy! Mummy, it's early! *(Mrs Lyons returning after having shown Mickey the door)* Mummy!
MRS LYONS	Edward. Where did you meet that boy?
EDDIE	*(Petulant)* At his house.
MRS LYONS	His second name ... his second name is Johnston ... isn't it Edward?
EDDIE	Yes! And I think you're very mean!
MRS LYONS	I've told you never to go where that boy lives.
EDDIE	But why?
MRS LYONS	Because ... because you're not the same as him. You're not! Do you understand?
EDDIE	No! No I don't understand ... And I hate you!
	(Instinctively she whacks him across the head but is immediately appalled)
MRS LYONS	Edward, Edward ... *(Pulling him to her, cradling him)*

Line numbers: 95, 100, 105, 110, 115

Edward you must understand, it's for your own good. It's only because I love you, Edward.

EDDIE   *(Breaking away. Complete rage)* You don't! If you loved me you'd let me go out with Mickey because he's my best friend. I like him more than you.

Activities

Ernie's Incredible Illucinations (page 68)

A key skill in writing scripts for performance is, of course, maintaining the attention of the audience. This can be done in many different ways, e.g:

- shock/surprise
- humour
- empathy (i.e. relating to people on the stage and their lives).

Sometimes, it is a question of taking the ordinary and turning it upside down, thus creating some – or all – of the above.

Making

In groups, read through the script on pages 68–73, and then discuss these questions:

- What two everyday situations are shown in this section of the play?
- How does the writer make them unusual, or different?

(Think about how the scene changes in the doctor's room; think about what happens at Ernie's house.)

Performing

Now, in your groups, work on a performance of the *opening* of this extract (down to Dad's line – *I'm blowed if I'm going to Birmingham. Even for United.)* Concentrate on showing the *transition* (change) from the doctor's surgery to Ernie's house.

Look carefully at the way the writer has helped you perform this transition with his stage directions.

Responding

Now write your own simple scene: a boy or girl your age is sitting at a bus stop, or train station, chatting with a friend about school and a history lesson, when suddenly the scene transforms into the boy/girl going back in time.

Use stage directions, and the same setting (i.e. the bus stop/train station) but transform it into a scene from the past.

Eclipse (page 74)

Think carefully about how you *interpret* Simon Armitage's language. On the one hand, this is a play about children ganging up on a blind boy, but the poetic way it is composed makes some of the lines lyrical and beautiful. You might want to consider performing this almost as if it is like an enchantment – as though the characters were under a spell.

Making

In pairs, prepare a short performance of the section of the script from Lucy saying, *But listen, what can you hear now?* down to *You're absolutely ultra-sonic* (lines 43–66).

Think carefully about how Midnight is standing. Is Lucy behind him? Whispering in his ear? Standing at a distance? Consider how you can *juxtapose* different images – that is, place two contrasting images or positionings of characters on stage in order to create an effect. For example, Lucy could come across rather like a puppet master, or the other children could be like a Greek chorus, watching and judging.

Focus in particular on lines that the speakers can savour and enjoy, to bring out the poetry, e.g:

- *… a cat licking its lips …*
- *… The wind playing the twine like a harp …*

Performing

Perform the suggested section in pairs.

Responding

Draw a simple plan of where Lucy and Midnight are standing on your 'stage' or acting space. Use the diagram on the next page to help you. You can show any movements with arrows and annotate with a line reference.

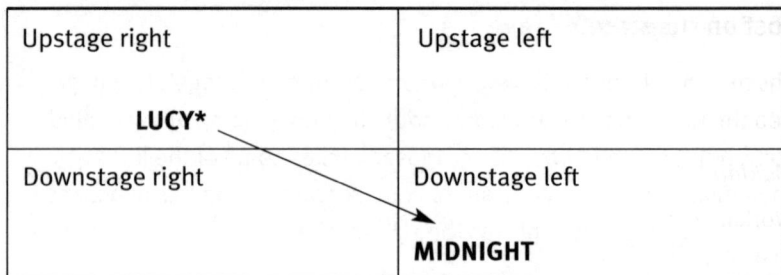

Upstage right	Upstage left
LUCY*	
Downstage right	Downstage left **MIDNIGHT**

AUDIENCE

Diagram example:

*moves closer, stands behind him on line *'What else? The boy with the kite?'*

Lost on the streets (page 79)

These two scenes are made up of encounters between Mariza and two people living on the streets – who react to her in different ways.

Making

Work in a small group. One of you should play the part of a newcomer to a city. All you want is to find an address – 13 Grange Avenue – the address of a distant relative. The other members of the group take on the roles of different people in the city: a police officer, a homeless person, a business man or woman, a café owner, etc. Each one is more interested in their own life and problems than in helping you. Improvise the arrival of the newcomer, and their (brief) encounters with each person.

Consider the *characterisation* of the different people and how it can be expressed in the way they speak, e.g:

Business person: Look, I'm doing lunch with the MD at one; I really can't factor you into my plans ...

Performing

Practise your improvisation, and add an appropriate ending to it – perhaps the newcomer finds 13 Grange Avenue – who is there? Is it whom – or what – they expected to find?

Next, perform the whole piece. Ensure that the encounters are relatively brief, but that the newcomer's sense of alienation is shown.

Responding

Now, turn your group work into a written script (written by you as an individual). Use *Lost on the streets* as a model for your work.

Characterisation can be aided by:

- brief but helpful stage directions *(e.g. He speaks accusingly)*
- appropriate language/speech *(I ... I ... I'm looking for my mum)*.

Finally, look again at *Lost on the streets*. How does the Old Woman's reaction to Mariza differ from that of Marcelo, the boy in the box?

Sparkleshark (page 85)

Making

When creating characters and locations in scripts, writers vary in the amount of information given to the director or actor. Shakespeare gives virtually nothing. However, Philip Ridley is quite different.

1. Look at the opening scene directions to *Sparkleshark* on page 85. Draw up a table like the one below and make notes on the things we find out about Jake.

Age	
Clothes, etc.	
Items belonging to him	
Looks and behaviour	*Slightly built*
Any other information	

2. Now write your own introductory stage direction for a character at the start of the play. You will also need to give some detailed information about the location, which is an old warehouse.

Your character can be any age, sex ... or creature! However, you *must* give as many details as Philip Ridley does. At this point, do not write any speech.

Performing

Now share with a friend the character you have created. Then, working together, improvise the meeting of your two characters at the old warehouse. You can either improvise without preparation, or you can decide the following things in advance:

*   whether one arrives first
*   if one of your characters is 'at home' in the warehouse
*   why they are there – or arrive there
*   how they get on.

Responding

When you have finished your improvisation, discuss with your friend how well the characters were established: was it clear why the characters were there, what sort of person/creature they were, etc?

My Mother Said I Never Should (page 91)

What makes this such an extraordinary piece of drama is the way the writer, Charlotte Keatley, takes quite an ordinary, everyday thing – children playing, talking about their parents, etc. – and turns it on its head. The children are played by adults, four different generations of the same family. In other words, children who could never meet in real life.

Making

The ritual and language of children's games are at the heart of this extract. Find examples from the extract (pages 91–95) of *typical* things the children do, and copy and complete the table below. There may be several examples for each one (some have been added for you).

Typical thing	Evidence/example in script
Rhymes/songs	
Ways of behaving (check stage directions)	*squirming*
Ways of speaking	*'Shut up, baby.'*
What they're interested in	

Performing

Work on a performance of the script. It doesn't matter if boys are playing girls' parts, as the play is not 'naturalistic'.

Try to get the moves and gestures of children of this age. It is also important that you consider the *intention* of the writer: does she want us to find the children ridiculous? Does she want us to recognise ourselves in what we watch? Does she want to show children as cruel and unpleasant – and shock us in some way?

Responding

When you perform your group's version of the scene to the rest of the class, or another group, try using a form of Forum Theatre to help develop your skills. What this means is that as you watch another group's performance you stop the action at some point, and if there is something that can be improved – or done in a different way – the person from the watching group swaps with the performer and takes over for a line or two – or more.

Using this method, evaluate your own performance and those of others. How close did you/they come to a way a child moves and speaks?

Blood Brothers (page 96)

The extract begins shortly after the two main characters have met for the first time, and has great emotional impact when Edward meets his real mother and then returns home, to be followed by Mickey. But a great deal of what interests the audience revolves around *dramatic irony*.

Dramatic irony refers to situations when characters or the audience have 'secret knowledge' about other characters or events. The two scenes on pages 96–101 become compelling because *we* (the audience) know they are actual brothers.

- How do the two mothers react differently to the appearance of the boys?
- What lines have particular impact because of dramatic irony?

Making

Invent a simple storyline around an event that creates dramatic irony. Once you have come up with your idea, describe what happens – and how the situation is resolved (for good or bad). Here are two possibilities:

- *A debt collector/loan shark visits a house to repossess items. He doesn't realise he is related to the person who lives there.*
- *A man and woman have secretly married. The woman's parents line up a different potential husband for her.*

Think of *five scenes* in which the story is told, e.g:

Scene 1:   *Man and woman at registry office marrying.*
Scene 2:   *Parents at home discussing potential husbands.*

In each case, there will need to be a scene when the audience (and/or another character on stage) sees the truth of what is happening as in Scene 1.

Performing and responding

Write your script and, as you do so, be quite clear about your own intentions. Are you trying to use irony to show people's stupidity, or to demonstrate how the world can conspire against them, whatever they do? Then perform your script. Afterwards, consider how well the dramatic irony worked.

- Did it create tension for the audience?
- Did it create humour? (It often does.)
- Most importantly, did it have the effect *you* intended?

Development and extension

Several of the extracts in this chapter deal with children's worlds – the games they play; the rituals; the ways they speak.

Take **two** of the following extracts: *My Mother Said I Never Should*, *Eclipse* and *Blood Brothers*, and write a commentary on both, comparing the similarities and differences in their treatment of childhood. Focus on the children's language and behaviour.

You may wish to use the writing frame below to help you.

The two script extracts are similar because they both deal with _____

In the first extract, we see _____

while in the second _____

Examples of children's language in the first are _____

This can also be seen in the second extract, in which _____

_____

As for the behaviour of the children, we can see that in

_____ *and, in the second* _____

However, there are differences too. Although one extract shows

_____

the other doesn't. Instead, it _____

To sum up, I think _____ *gives a really good idea of how children behave and speak.*

Child's play

Create your own longer script that deals with children, their language, behaviour, rituals, games, etc.

Choose **one** of the following scenarios:

- a gang daring a girl/boy to do something
- children walking to school through a wood, reputed to be haunted
- children exploring an upstairs room in a house on someone's birthday.

Make sure you include some or all of the following:

1. Scene details

Example: *A children's room. Dusty wallpaper, and a teddy on the floor with one eye missing. A mobile on the ceiling of faded butterflies swings slowly in the breeze from the cracked window pane.*

2. Typical child's language

Example: **Katie:** *I'm not gonna be your best friend anymore!*

Emma: *I'm telling my mum.*

3. Children's behaviour

Example: **Katie** *(bangs fists on the floor)*: *I hate you! Hate you!*

4. Ritual, games, songs

Example: *Bets, oaths, secrets, messages, naughtiness, rhymes, chants, etc.*

When you have written your script (or while developing it) practise and perform it with a group of friends, taking their input on board, and – where necessary – adapting and changing the script so that it works even more powerfully.

You could combine with other groups or individuals to create a 'Child's play' show in which part or all of your script is shown with other people's.

Your 'Child's play' show could:

1   start with *all* actors on stage, frozen in time, as children doing various activities

2   move into a short first scene involving a small group of children

3   use music or song to bridge into another scene and subsequent scenes

4   end with all actors on stage, but now as adults in 'grown-up' situations.

Chapter 4: Interpretations

The same play can be performed in different ways, and seen in different ways. One member of the audience might think a play is tragic, whilst another might find it ridiculous. This chapter explores the different ways the same ideas or stories can be interpreted, by actors, directors, or audiences. Shakespeare is well-represented and there is a range of other scripts for you to explore as well.

In this chapter you will:
- explore how single words or phrases can be interpreted in different ways
- look at how writers can change the way we see well-known characters
- study texts in which writers have updated or adapted familiar ideas
- compare the presentation of the same play or performance by different people.

Beatrice and Benedick (from *Much Ado About Nothing*)

William Shakespeare

This famous comedy by William Shakespeare concerns a lord, Benedick, who in support of the Prince of Aragon, Don Pedro, falls out with Beatrice, niece of Leonato, the Governor of Sicily. At a masked ball, Benedick, in disguise, speaks with Beatrice, who says what she thinks of him (Benedick) – most of it not very pleasant. Later, in Act 2 Scene 1, Benedick talks with Don Pedro. As you look at this scene, think about how Benedick might speak – does he mean what he says? Is he really hurt by her? Use the activities on pages 141–142 to help you.

Characters in order of appearance (3)

Don Pedro
Benedick
Beatrice

DON PEDRO The Lady Beatrice hath a quarrel to you: the gentleman that danced with her told her she is much wronged by you.

BENEDICK O, she **misused** me past the endurance of a block! an
5 oak but with one green leaf on it would have answered her; my very **visor** began to assume life and scold with her. She told me, not thinking I had been myself, that I was the prince's jester, that I was duller than a great thaw; huddling jest upon jest with such
10 impossible **conveyance** upon me that I stood like a man at a mark, with a whole army shooting at me. She speaks **poniards**, and every word stabs: if her

misused abused
visor mask
conveyance skill/pace (in speaking)
poniard small, slim dagger

breath were as terrible as her terminations, there
were no living near her; she would infect to the north

15 star. I would not marry her, though she were
endowed with all that Adam had left him before he
transgressed: she would have made Hercules have
turned spit, yea, and have cleft his club to make the
fire too. Come, talk not of her: you shall find her the

20 infernal **Ate** in good apparel. I would to God some
scholar would conjure her; for certainly, while she is
here, a man may live as quiet in hell as in a sanctuary;
and people sin upon purpose, because they would go
thither; so, indeed, all disquiet, horror, and

25 **perturbation** follows her.

DON PEDRO   Look, here she comes.

Re-enter Claudio, Beatrice, Hero, and Leonato.

BENEDICK   Will your grace command me any service to the
world's end? I will go on the slightest errand now to

30 the Antipodes that you can devise to send me on; I
will fetch you a tooth-picker now from the furthest
inch of Asia, bring you the length of **Prester John**'s
foot, fetch you a hair off the great **Cham**'s beard, do
you any embassage to the Pigmies, rather than hold

35 three words' conference with this harpy. You have no
employment for me?

DON PEDRO   None, but to desire your good company.

BENEDICK   O God, sir, here's a dish I love not: I cannot endure
my Lady Tongue. *Exit*

---

transgressed   sinned
Ate   Greek goddess of vengeance
perturbation   disturbance
Prester John   a legendary foreign king
Cham   an Asian lord/king

40	**DON PEDRO**	Come, lady, come; you have lost the heart of Signior Benedick.
	BEATRICE	Indeed, my lord, he lent it me awhile; and I gave him use for it, a double heart for his single one: marry, once before he won it of me with false dice, therefore
45		your grace may well say I have lost it.
	DON PEDRO	You have put him down lady, you have put him down.
	BEATRICE	So I would not he should do me, my lord …

Stone

Edward Bond

Many stories – especially myths and fairy tales – have simple plots, but have dark and powerful undercurrents: fear of strangers, hatred of a jealous parent, envy and desire. Some modern writers, like Edward Bond, present us with a simple tale in simple language, but add an element that is threatening, or slightly strange and off-key. Read this extract, in which one man asks another to run an errand for him – but what else is going on? And who is to be trusted? Use the activities on pages 143–144 to help you.

Characters in order of appearance (2)

Mason
Man

Scene One

Road. Empty stage. A young man comes on. He is eager and relaxed. A middle-aged man comes on. He is quiet and efficient and wears a business suit. He is a mason.

	MASON	Where are you off to?
5	MAN	*(half smiles)* Why?
	MASON	You're not lost?
	MAN	No, I'm going to find a job and make my place in the world.
	MASON	Good luck.
10	MAN	Thanks. *(Smiles)* I left home this morning. My father and mother can't keep me now.
	MASON	What work d'you want?

MAN	I could learn to do almost anything.
MASON	What did your parents give you to take out in the world?
15 **MAN**	*(touches his pocket. Half smiles)* Something.
MASON	Generous!
MAN	They didn't have much but they wouldn't let me go empty handed.
MASON	How much?
20 **MAN**	*(cunning)* Ha-ha.
MASON	Do I look like a thief?
MAN	You might be a clever thief.
MASON	I'm weaker than you. You could knock me down.
MAN	That's true.
25 **MASON**	But you wouldn't.
MAN	Why not?
MASON	I'm very rich. But I don't carry money on me. So I agree: it's not worth knocking me down. Congratulations on changing your mind.
30 **MAN**	I didn't change my mind! I never meant to knock you down.
MASON	No? You'll find – out in the world – it's better to expect the worst. *(Takes out a pistol)* Like this.
MAN	*(shortly)* O.
35 **MASON**	How much?
MAN	Not much.
MASON	How much?

MAN	Seven gold talents.
MASON	*(blandly)* Seven. *(Jerks the pistol)* Show me.

40   *The Man takes out seven gold coins.*

MASON	Pockets out.

The Man pulls out his pockets. They are empty.

MASON	Hand it over. *(He names each coin as it is put into his hands)* Prudence, soberness, courage, justice, honesty, love –

45   *(The Man drops a coin)* Pick it up. *(The Man picks it up and gives it to the Mason)* Hope. Now what will you do?

MAN	I won't go home.
MASON	They can't afford to take you back.
MAN	I'd be ashamed to ask them. I wasted their money. They

50   worked so hard for it.

MASON	They should have warned you about thieves.
MAN	They did. But the sun was shining and I thought no one would spoil a day like this by stealing. I shall go to the police.

55   **MASON**   Then I shall have to shoot you. You're spoiling my day too!

MAN	*(annoyed with himself)* Blast.
MASON	You'll really have to control your tongue. *(Sighs. Shakes his head)* Shooting people works out expensive.

60   Fortunately I don't have to shoot you. The police are far too busy to worry about your seven talents!

Mason gives the money back to the Man.

MAN	O. *(Puts the money in his pocket grumpily)* Thanks.

MASON	Let me give you a job.
65 MAN	Don't pull my leg.
MASON	What?
MAN	You won't give me a job.
MASON	Why not?
70 MAN	You wouldn't trust me. You made me look a fool. I didn't show much sense did I?
MASON	*(nodding)* Yes, you'll suit me very well.
MAN	It must be such hard work you can't get anyone else to do it.
MASON	No, it's the sort of job people queue up for.
75 MAN	What's the catch?
MASON	Can't someone just want to help you?
MAN	No.
MASON	Your parents did.
MAN	That's different.
80 MASON	You bring out my paternal instinct.
MAN	What job is it?
MASON	*(takes a stone from his pocket)* Here's a stone. No more than a pebble really. Take it to my house.
MAN	That stone?
85 MASON	My house is along the road.
MAN	Why don't you take it?
MASON	My business takes me the other way.

	MAN	Let me look. *(The Mason holds the stone on the flat of his palm)* Is it an ordinary stone?
90	MASON	It's just as you see it.
	MAN	Why d'you want it?
	MASON	I'm a stone mason. No doubt I see more in it than you do.
	MAN	*(takes the stone)* It looks ordinary.
	MASON	I told you.
95	MAN	How far is your house?
	MASON	Quite a way. You'll come to it. Tell them I sent you.
	MAN	Why an ordinary stone?
	MASON	It could be the ordinariness that interests me.
	MAN	And wages?
100	MASON	You're paid when you deliver the goods.
	MAN	How much?
	MASON	That depends how quickly you deliver them.
	MAN	*(returns the stone)* That's the catch.
	MASON	*(shrugs)* I don't pay in advance.
105	MAN	I don't work till I'm paid.
	MASON	You won't find an easier job.
	MAN	I don't trust you.
	MASON	I want to help you. But I won't give money away. That ruins people, especially the young. Encourages
110		scrounging. Deliver this stone – that's not much to ask. I could have robbed you. Instead I offer you an easy job – and you say you don't trust me! I'll be on my way. *(Starts to go)*

MAN	Well – *(Stops short)*
115 MASON	*(turning round)* Yes?
MAN	How will I know your house?
MASON	It's by a stone-yard.
MAN	Suppose someone offers me a better job?
MASON	They'll offer to carry *you*?
120 MAN	I might get lost or fed up.
MASON	Now you see the place of trust. I have to trust you. You could throw my stone away anytime. But I trust you. Within reason. That's why I don't pay till you deliver the goods.
125 MAN	I see.
MASON	And you have to trust me. Within reason. I say wait to be paid – but I ask so little. If I'd said murder your grandmother – I'd have asked too much. You'd expect to be paid first. Rightly. Or if I'd said sell your soul. Kill your brothers. Swallow the ocean. Then you wouldn't want to be paid at all! – because you're a good lad and you'd rather live by your talents. While they last. So I ask little: carry a stone. And I only ask that because it's the easiest way I can help you without offending my principles. It would be very odd if you said no.
MAN	Yes, I see.
MASON	So you enter my employ?
MAN	Er yes.
140 MASON	*(raises finger)* Call me sir now you're one of mine.
MAN	Yes sir.
MASON	*(gives the stone to the Man)* Excellent.

Rosencrantz and Guildenstern Are Dead

Tom Stoppard

It isn't only actors and directors who interpret plays. Sometimes writers take established plays, and put their own stamp on them, often by retelling them with a new focus, or creating new stories from the germ of the original. Tom Stoppard's play is based on two minor characters from Shakespeare's *Hamlet*. In the original play, they are given the job of tricking Hamlet into going to England with them, by ship, where they will betray him to the King, and he will be executed. Hamlet finds out, however. In Stoppard's version, we see – or more accurately – hear, the two men on board ship, bound for England. Read through the extract then complete the activities on pages 145–146.

Characters in order of appearance (2)

Guildenstern
Rosencrantz

Act Three

Opens in pitch darkness. Soft sea sounds.

After several seconds of nothing, a voice from the dark.

	GUIL	Are you there?
	ROS	Where?
5	GUIL	*(bitterly)* A flying start …
		Pause.
	ROS	Is that you?
	GUIL	Yes.
	ROS	How do you know?
10	GUIL	*(explosion)* Oh-for-God's-sake!

ROS	We're not finished, then?
GUIL	Well, we're here, aren't we?
ROS	Are we? I can't see a thing.
GUIL	You can still *think*, can't you?

15 ROS   I think so.

GUIL   You can still *talk*.

ROS   What should I say?

GUIL   Don't bother. You can *feel*, can't you?

ROS   Ah! There's life in me yet!

20 GUIL   What are you feeling?

ROS   A leg. Yes, it feels like my leg.

GUIL   How does it feel?

ROS   Dead.

GUIL   Dead?

25 ROS   *(panic)* I can't feel a thing!

GUIL   Give it a pinch! *(Immediately he yelps)*

ROS   Sorry.

GUIL   Well, that's cleared that up.

30 *Longer pause: the sound builds a little and identifies itself – the sea. Ship timbers, wind in the rigging, and then shouts of sailors calling obscure but inescapably nautical instructions from all directions, far and near: A short list:*

Hard a larboard!
Let go the stays!
35 Reef down me hearties!

Is that you, cox'n?
Hel-llo! Is that you?
Hard a port!
Easy as she goes!

40   Keep her steady on the lee!
Haul away, lads!
(Snatches of sea shanty maybe.)
Fly the jib!
Tops'l up, me maties!

45   *When the point has been well made and more so ...*

ROS   We're on a boat. *(Pause)* Dark, isn't it?

GUIL   Not for night.

ROS   No, not for *night*.

GUIL   Dark for day.

50   *Pause.*

ROS   Oh yes, it's dark for *day*.

GUIL   We must have gone north, of course.

ROS   Off course?

GUIL   Land of the midnight sun, that is.

55 ROS Of course.

        Some sailor sounds.

        A lantern is lit upstage – in fact by Hamlet.

        The stage lightens disproportionately – enough to see:

        Rosencrantz and Guildenstern sitting downstage.

60   *Vague shapes of rigging, etc., behind.*

ROS   I think it's getting light.

	GUIL	Not for night.
	ROS	This far north.
	GUIL	Unless we're off course.
65	ROS	*(small pause)* Of course.

A better light – Lantern? Moon? ... Light.

Revealing, among other things, three large man-sized casks on deck, upended, with lids. Spaced but in line. Behind and above – a gaudy striped umbrella, on a pole stuck into the deck, tilted so that we do not see behind it – one of those huge six-foot-diameter jobs. Still dim upstage. Rosencrantz and Guildenstern still facing front.

	ROS	Yes, it's lighter than it was. It'll be night soon. This far north. *(Dolefully)* I suppose we'll have to go to sleep. *(He yawns and stretches)*
	GUIL	Where?
	ROS	What?
	GUIL	I thought you – *(Relapses)* I've lost all capacity for disbelief. I'm not sure that I could even rise to a little gentle scepticism.

Pause.

	ROS	Well, shall we stretch our legs?
	GUIL	I don't feel like stretching my legs.
	ROS	I'll stretch them for you, if you like.
85	GUIL	No.
	ROS	We could stretch each other's. That way we wouldn't have to go anywhere.

	GUIL	*(pause)* No, somebody might come in.
	ROS	In where?
90	GUIL	Out here.
	ROS	In out here?
	GUIL	On deck.

Rosencrantz considers the floor: slaps it.

	ROS	Nice bit of planking, that.
95	GUIL	Yes, I'm very fond of boats myself. I like the way they're – contained. You don't have to worry about which way to go, or whether to go at all – the question doesn't arise, because you're on a *boat,* aren't you? Boats are safe areas in the game of tag … the players will hold their positions
100		until the music starts … I think I'll spend most of my life on boats.
	ROS	Very healthy.

Rosencrantz inhales with expectation, exhales – with boredom.
Guildenstern stands up and looks over the audience.

105	GUIL	One is free on a boat. For a time. Relatively.
	ROS	What's it like?
	GUIL	Rough.

Rosencrantz joins him. They look out over the audience.

| | ROS | I think I'm going to be sick. |

East is East

Ayub Khan-Din

The play from which this extract comes is set in the 1970s. Ella is a
white woman born in the UK. Her husband, George, is from Pakistan.
He has arranged a marriage for two of their sons with two girls from
the Shah family, despite opposition from Ella. In fact, he has already
violently beaten Ella when she stood up to him about it. George is
close to breaking point, pulled between two conflicting cultures. Read
through the extract then complete the activities on pages 147–148.

Characters in order of appearance (8)

Ella Khan (mother, aged 46)
Meenah Khan (daughter, aged 16)
Abdul Khan (son, aged 23)
Saleem Khan (son, aged 18)
George Khan (father, aged 55)
Tariq Khan (son, aged 21)
Sajit Khan (son, aged 12) (doesn't speak)
Maneer Khan (son, aged 19)

	ELLA	You ought to be ashamed George, you're not getting these lads married, you're selling them off to the highest bidder. Who's gonna get Meenah? Someone with double glazing and a detached house!

5 *George grabs Ella, and pushes her to the floor, he starts to hit her.*

MEENAH Maam! Maam! Abdul stop him!

*Saleem and Tariq run over to try and stop him, Maneer
grabs Ella and tries to pull her away. Sajit takes off his*
10 *coat, runs over, and starts to hit George with it.*

ABDUL	Dad! *(He grabs George and pushes him against the wall)* Get off her, stop it.
SALEEM	Smack him one Abdul!
ABDUL	Dad, if you touch her again I swear I'll kill you!
15 **GEORGE**	You don't talk ...
ABDUL	No dad, it's over, alright, it's finished!

Sajit is still hitting him with his parka.

ABDUL	Sajit stop it!

Sajit carries on hitting George.

20 **ABDUL**	I said stop it!

Sajit stops and runs off to the shed crying. Pause. There's just the sound of Ella, crying. The others help her into a chair.

ABDUL	Just calm down dad, alright?

George starts to cry.

25 **GEORGE**	I only try to help you son ...

LATER ...

Ella goes to the shed.

SALEEM	She's just gonna leave it, isn't she?
TARIQ	What else do you expect her to do?
30 **SALEEM**	She'll just let him walk back in here after what he's done?
MEENAH	He did after **Nazir** left didn't he.
SALEEM	So you're just gonna sit there, with your heads in the sand, until it happens again?

Nazir *another son, who has been disowned by George for becoming a hairdresser, and not marrying.*

35	ABDUL	No one's hiding. Me mam's just trying to hold her family together.
	SALEEM	Family! This isn't a family! Normal families sit down and talk. We say something out of line, me dad hits us and that's it.
40	ABDUL	It's not as simple as that, and you know it.
	SALEEM	She should divorce him.
	ABDUL	You're all missing the point, have you not thought that she might love him?
	MEENAH	Me dad?
45	ABDUL	What else do you think has kept them together for so long? We're the cause of most of the arguments between them, 'cause she always takes our side.
	TARIQ	So what do we do now, Abdul?
50	ABDUL	Try and make things easier for her, don't make her job any harder than it is. It's me dad that's gonna have to change.
	MANEER	He was only trying to show us our culture.
55	ABDUL	He's got no right to tell us what our culture should be, he lost that when he settled here and married me mam.
	MEENAH	God Abdul, you sound dead different.
	SALEEM	Say that when you get married off.
60	ABDUL	That's not gonna happen to her, it's not gonna happen to anyone who doesn't want it. I'm telling you, things are gonna be different round here.

He picks up Sajit's coat from the floor and goes to the yard.

Cyrano de Bergerac

Edmond Rostand

This French play has been produced in many forms, including the Hollywood comedy *Roxanne*, starring Steve Martin and Daryl Hannah. (In that version the Cyrano character and Christian are firefighters in a small US town.) In this scene the handsome, but not very educated, Christian is trying out his romantic skills on the woman he loves, following a letter written and sent on his behalf by Cyrano. Read through the extract then complete the activities on page 149.

Characters in order of appearance (3)

Roxane
Christian
Cyrano

ROXANE   *(as the guests disappear down the street, she turns to Christian)*

Is that you, Christian ? Let us stay
Here, in the twilight. They are gone. The air
5   Is fragrant. We shall be alone. Sit down
There – so …

(they sit on the bench)

Now tell me things.

CHRISTIAN   *(after a silence)*

I love you.

10   ROXANE   *(closes her eyes)*

Yes,

Speak to me about love …

CHRISTIAN   I love you.

ROXANE   Now,

Be eloquent! …

| 15 | CHRISTIAN | I love – |

ROXANE *(opens her eyes)*

You have your theme –
Improvise! Rhapsodise!

CHRISTIAN I love you so!

20 ROXANE Of course. And then? …

CHRISTIAN And then … Oh, I should be
So happy if you loved me too! Roxane,
Say that you love me too!

ROXANE *(making a face)*

25 I ask for cream
You give me milk and water. Tell me first
A little, how you love me.

CHRISTIAN Very much.

ROXANE Oh – tell me how you *feel*!

30 CHRISTIAN *(coming nearer, and devouring her with his eyes)*

Your throat … If only
I might … kiss it –

ROXANE Christian!

CHRISTIAN I love you so!

35 ROXANE *(makes as if to rise)*
Again?

CHRISTIAN *(desperately, restraining her)*
No, not again – I do not love you –

ROXANE *(settles back)*
40 That is better …

CHRISTIAN I adore you!

ROXANE	Oh! *(rises and moves away)*
CHRISTIAN	I know; I grow absurd.

45 ROXANE *(coldly)*
                    And that displeases me
As much as if you had grown ugly.

CHRISTIAN   I –

ROXANE Gather your dreams together into words!

50 CHRISTIAN I love –

ROXANE   I know; you love me. Adieu.
(She goes to the house)

CHRISTIAN   No,
But wait – please – let me – I was going to say –

55 ROXANE *(pushes the door open)*
That you adore me. Yes; I know that too.
No! ... Go away! ...
(she goes in and shuts the door in his face)

CHRISTIAN   I ... I ...

60 CYRANO *(enters)*
                                        A great success!

CHRISTIAN Help me!

CYRANO   Not I.

CHRISTIAN   I cannot live unless
65 She loves me – now, this moment!

CYRANO   How the devil
Am I to teach you now – this moment?

CHRISTIAN *(catches him by the arm)*

                                    – Wait! –

70   Look! Up there ! – Quick –

            The light shows in Roxane's window.

CYRANO   Her window –

CHRISTIAN   *(wailing)*
                                    I shall die!

75 CYRANO Less noise!

CHRISTIAN   Oh, I –

CYRANO   It does seem fairly dark –

CHRISTIAN   *(excitedly)*
            Well? – Well? – Well? –

80 CYRANO   Let us try what can be done;
            It is more than you deserve – stand over there,
            Idiot – there ! – before the balcony –
            Let me stand underneath. I'll whisper you
            What to say.

Ti-Jean and his Brothers

Derek Walcott

This play by the acclaimed poet and playwright Derek Walcott is set in a land like the one of his birth, St Lucia. It opens with a prologue – a setting of the scene, introduced by the creatures of the forest, and features song, dance, music, poetry and chanting ... as well as the odd bit of French, the language of the colonial rulers. Read through the extract then complete the activities on page 150.

Characters in order of appearance (6)

Cricket
Frog
Firefly (doesn't speak)
Bird
Gros Jean (doesn't speak)
Mi-Jean (doesn't speak)

Prologue

Evening. Rain. The heights of a forest. A Cricket, a Frog, a Firefly, a Bird. Left, a hut with bare table, an empty bowl, stools. The Mother waiting.

FROG	Greek-croak, Greek-croak.
CRICKET	Greek-croak, Greek-croak.

5 *The others join.*

FROG	*(sneezing)* **Aeschylus** me!
	All that rain and no moon tonight.
CRICKET	The moon always there even fighting the rain
	Creek-crak, it is cold, but the moon always there
10	... And Ti-Jean in the moon just like the story.

Bird passes.

Aeschylus Ancient Greek dramatist

CRICKET	Before you fly home, listen,
	The cricket cracking a story
	A story about the moon.

15 FROG   If you look in the moon,
Though no moon is here tonight,
There is a man, no, a boy,
Bent by a weight of **faggots**
He carried on his shoulder,
20   A small dog trotting with him.
That is **Ti**-Jean the hunter,
He got the heap of sticks
From the old man of the forest
They calling Papa Bois,
25   Because he beat the devil,
God put him in that height
To be the sun's right hand
And light the evil dark,
But as the bird so ignorant
30   I will start the tale truly.

Music.

Well, one time it had a mother,
That mother had three sons.
The first son was **Gros** Jean.
35   That son he was the biggest,
His arm was hard as iron,
But he was very stupid.

*Enter Gros Jean, a bundle of faggots in one hand, an axe over
his shoulder, moving in an exaggerated march to music. The
40   creatures laugh.*

---

faggots firewood
Ti short for French *petit* 'small'
Gros French 'large' or 'big'

FROG	The name of the second son.
	They was calling him **Mi**-Jean,
	In size, the second biggest,
	So only half as stupid; now,
45	He was a fisherman, but
	Always studying book, and
	What a fisherman; for
	When he going and fish,
	Always forgetting the bait,
50	So between de bait and debate …

| CRICKET | *Mi boug qui tail cooyon!* |
| | (Look man who was a fool!) |

*Roll of drums. Comic **quatro**, martial.*

Enter Mi-Jean from the opposite side, carrying a book in one
55 *hand and a fishing net over his shoulder. Halfway across the*
stage he flings the net casually, still reading.

| BIRD | How poor their mother was? |

Sad music on flute.

FROG	Oh that was poverty, bird!
60	Old hands dried up like claws
	Heaping old sticks on sticks,
	Too weak to protect her nest.
	Look, the four of that family

Light shows the hut.

65	Lived in a little house,
	Made up of wood and thatch,
	On the forehead of the mountain,
	Where night and day was rain,

Mi French 'middle sized' or 'half'
quatro four (here, probably a four-beat piece of music or drum-beat)

Mist, cloud white as cotton
70   Caught in the dripping branches;
Where sometimes it was so cold
The frog would stop its singing

The Frog stops. Five beats. Resumes.

The cricket would stop rattling
75   And the wandering firefly
That lights the tired woodsman
Home through the raining trees
Could not strike a damp light
To star the wanderer home!

80   *The music stops. The brothers Gros Jean and Mi-Jean put their*
arms around each other, and to heavy drums tramp home.

Activities

Beatrice and Benedick (page 116)

Making

1. Try saying the following line in different ways:

    'She said I was dull'

Try it:

- indignantly – you can't *believe* she said it
- angrily – how dare she?!
- upset – she's hurt your feelings
- jokily – it's not worth taking seriously.

Now say it any other way you can think of, e.g. try emphasising 'she' as if to say, 'How can someone as dull as her, accuse me?'

This is a modern version of a line from the extract said by Benedick, and it shows the difficulty of trying to interpret how someone is feeling. Although the lines seem to give clues, there is a lot of room for the actor's or director's own *interpretation* – their decision on how a part can be played.

2. Take Benedick's long speech on pages 116–117 starting 'O, she misused me ...' down to the line 'I would not marry her ... transgressed.' Don't worry too much about what it means, just try to come up with a way of saying the lines that fits the interpretation you want to give (i.e. angry, indignant, etc.).

To do this, focus on how you would say individual words, e.g. (through gritted teeth, shaking his fist in her direction offstage).

> 'I would not marry *her* ...' *(pauses and strides to front of stage, looking women in the audience up and down)* ... though she were endowed with all that Adam had left him before he transgressed ...'

Performing and responding

Look at different people's versions of Benedick's speech and examine how they have interpreted him. Of course, if you were studying the play as a whole, you would need to look at his behaviour elsewhere. For example, just before Don Pedro comes in, Benedick says, 'I'll be revenged ...' Does he mean this nastily, or is he already attracted to Beatrice?

Stone (page 119)

Many plays, like stories, as we have seen with some of the extracts in this collection, have stock features and conventions, whether it is the innocent hero who faces a terrible choice, or the evil villain hiding his or her real purposes. But in more modern plays, it's not always clear who the villain is – or how he or she should be played.

Making

What is *Stone* about? It certainly starts in a *conventional* way – like a fairy-tale.

1. Read the extract on pages 119–124 carefully with a partner, then answer the questions below.

a) How is the beginning of *Stone* like a fairy tale? Consider:

*   the language used
*   the setting
*   what the 'man' is doing.

b) How is it *different* from a traditional fairy tale? Consider:

*   obvious things, such as modern-day references
*   surprises in what happens in the story
*   the characters (Do we know whether the mason is good or bad? Would we know in a fairy tale?).

Performing and responding

It could be said that this play has a number of *themes* (though you would have to read it all to find out if they are consistent throughout). For example, some themes might be:

*   growing up
*   the loss of innocence
*   the importance (or lack of importance) of money
*   the value of things generally
*   parents and children.

Can you see evidence for any of these in the extract? Make brief notes on which of these themes seem relevant.

Then, consider how focusing on one of these themes might make you change your performance. For example, if this was a play about parents and children would this influence how the 'man' was played – i.e. more like a child?

Rosencrantz and Guildenstern Are Dead (page 125)

Taking a well-known story or tale, and giving it a new or unusual treatment, happens in all forms of writing: poetry, prose or drama. Even Shakespeare took old stories and added characters or changed the focus. Here, Tom Stoppard takes two less important characters from *Hamlet* and builds a play around a line near the end when their death is announced.

Making

Look at the characters of the two men in Stoppard's play on pages 125–129. In Shakespeare's *Hamlet* they are presented as agents of the king, ready to betray Hamlet (the play's main *protagonist*), possibly even former friends of Hamlet's, though he sees through them from the beginning.

What impression of them do we get here? Write some notes about how they behave and how they relate to each other.

- Are they sympathetic? (Would we, as an audience, like them?)
- Are they to be feared?
- Are they to be laughed at?

Find evidence for your impressions in the form of actual quotations or examples from the script, and include them in your notes. For example:

'They seem like a double act – a team – especially as they seem to echo one another's lines:

GUIL   Unless we're off course.

ROS   Of course.'

Performing

Take any well-known story or traditional tale and develop an improvisation based on it, but focused on minor characters. For example, it could be the two ugly sisters from *Cinderella*, but you would need to try to make them more real – less of a *caricature* (this means a character who has no depth – a bit like a cartoon cut-out, without real 'feelings').

Responding

Write the script of your tale. Have you succeeded in making it different from the original? Have you succeeded in shifting the focus from the main character to your character/s?

East is East (page 130)

Dramas and stories based around the idea of the arranged marriage
are centuries old, and range from fairy tales to modern sit-coms. In
this play, however, Ayub Khan-Din attempts to put his own stamp on
the issue – to interpret it in his own way. This is not a white outsider's
view of the situation, it is seen very much from within the family
(albeit it with a white mother).

Making

In small groups, discuss the following questions:

- How are we meant to view George (the father) in this extract? After
  all, he has tried to do what is acceptable to a Muslim community in
  terms of marrying off two of his sons. In this, Maneer supports him.
- Who takes control in this scene?
- Sajit has spent the entire play wearing his parka with the hood up,
  usually the butt of his brothers' and sister's jokes, and often
  confused and bewildered by the goings-on in the family. At the end
  of the play Sajit comes out of his hiding place and throws his
  parka away. What do you think this symbolises?

Performing

In groups, prepare and perform part, or all, of the extract. Think
carefully about how you can bring out the different characters in this
scene, through:

- tone of voice
- gesture/position
- facial expression.

Responding

Write a short piece in which you consider how the part of George
should be played. You will need to think about how he progresses
through a range of emotions:

- shame (at being shown up by Ella)

- anger
- violence
- confusion (when Abdul stands up to him)
- being upset.

Be very specific about how he might move and speak in each of these.

Cyrano de Bergerac (page 133)

Making

If you had to update this scene to a modern setting, how would you do it?

Christian has decided he doesn't need Cyrano's help in wooing Roxane, but as this scene shows, he does. She expects flowery, romantic words – not dull and repeated exclamations of 'I love you ...'.

Read through the scene on pages 133–136, and then work on an improvisation without the script, set in the present day. You must keep:

- the basic story
- the characters of the three main people involved.

But you can change the setting, the time and the characters' occupations, as Steve Martin did in his film version. For example:

- Cyrano could be a foreign football coach
- Roxane could be a young woman fan
- Christian could be a talented, good-looking young player (with few brains)
- the setting could be the street where Roxane lives, near the ground.

ROXANE	Wow. You've come to my house. Let's sit in the garden – away from the prying eyes of my family. Tell me what you're thinking ...
CHRIS	Err. You're great, like. Dead nice.

Performing

Perform your new version of the scene, trying to ensure you keep the basic story and characters as the original.

Responding

How successful was your improvisation? The original play is funny – but it is also sad. Cyrano really does love Roxane, but because of his looks he is sure she can never love him. Find out how the original play ends, and how Cyrano both gets what he wants – and loses it too.

Ti-Jean and his Brothers (page 137)

It is clear from the opening that this piece has a different cultural background from the other texts in this chapter. It was written by poet and playwright Derek Walcott, and reflects his roots in St Lucia.

Making

Read the extract on pages 137–140 again, and answer the following questions:

1. How does the opening recall a child's tale or story? What elements might you see in other traditional children's stories?

2. In the introduction to the play, Derek Walcott says he wanted to recreate the feel of 'those old country-firelight storytellers who frightened us all as children'. Why would such a story have been especially frightening in a Caribbean location?

3. There are also links with other forms of storytelling – especially the Greek use of a chorus. Who acts as the chorus in this play? What little references does the writer make to this at the start?

Performing

The play follows the conventions of many fairy tales and myths. Each brother in turn goes into the forest. He meets an Old Man who offers advice, and then the Devil in the form of a plantation owner for whom he is forced to work. If he loses his temper, the Devil destroys him. It is clear that the Old Man is not all he seems!

In a group, perform your own version of the opening, using the script. Consider:

• How the creatures and humans will move (in choreographed dance moves?).
• Whether to use costumes or masks for the animals, creatures etc.
• How lighting and music can contribute to your interpretation.

Responding

You probably have a good sense of the style and form of the piece now. Write down what you think might happen in the story, given what you know about similar children's tales. Compare your ideas with other people in your group and class. Select one idea (or a combination of ideas) and develop the rest of the play.

Development and extension

Comparing two presentations of the same play or performance

1. Watch two performances that arise from the same stimulus, or are based on the same script. As you watch them, make brief notes on the same issues:

The general tone/style of the two pieces	*lively, funny, dark, sad, etc.*
Which characters came over most strongly?	
Whether there was a dominant theme	*e.g. family, the power of envy*
How the same characters were portrayed	*i.e. in one as an evil villain, in the other, more sympathetically*
Whether the story was told in the same way	*i.e. the order of events*
The settings (if relevant)	*i.e. the same scenes, props, etc.*

2. Then write up your comparison. Use a variety of link words and connectives to ensure your analysis is clear, for example:

however, on the other hand, in contrast   to show differences

similarly, in the same way, also   to show similarities.

A simple tale

Another feature of many of the extracts in this section is the way playwrights had taken some quite basic story ideas and invigorated them by making them humorous or down-to-earth and/or adding something sinister and less easy to pin down.

For example, in *Stone*, what are we to make of Mason? He accosts the Man, pulls a gun on him, steals his money, then gives it back. Then he offers the man a job, but the job seems strange – to take a stone to Mason's house.

Is he a villain with some plan in mind – or a kindly stranger, helping the 'Man' out?

1. Write your own very simple tale, involving not more than three people. It should use very simple language.

It should start with an encounter between two people who have not met before. But the play should be slightly bizarre; or the characters should act in unexpected ways. For example:

WOMAN   *(in hospital bed)* Who are you?

MAN   I'm a visitor.

WOMAN   I can see that. What do you want?

MAN   I want you to tell me a secret.

WOMAN   A secret? What secret?

MAN   How do I know till you tell me?

2. Perform your play. Are you able to make it simple – and slightly surreal and weird at the same time?

If you are not sure what style to adopt, re-read *Stone* and try to imitate the use of language and speech you find there.

Chapter 5: Reflections

This chapter is all about the ways in which you think, talk and write about the drama you have created or seen. This is a vital part of drama work. It is what professional actors, directors, film and theatre reviewers do when they consider their own work. But, as you will see from the first extract, the lines between play and reality are often blurred.

In this chapter you will:
- consider the place of drama in 'real life'
- discover how film and theatre reviews are written
- explore the connection between characters' and the actors' own lives
- look at how students like yourself have analysed their own work and performances
- learn about effective ways of describing your own work and that of others.

Black Truth

Brenda Agard

Children's play – a form of early drama – is central to most of our lives as we grow up. The chance to become someone else, to try out other lives, to act out fantasies and stories, is a necessary part of understanding who we are and what we want. However, as in this poem, the barrier between play and reality can be a very thin one indeed. Read through the poem then complete the activities on pages 176–177.

The wounded were coming
in their hundreds it
seemed. The nurses
would patch them up
5 send them back out
to the front

But they would come back
in their hundreds it
seemed.

10 The bell rang.

Come afternoon the
wounded were coming
in their hundreds it
seemed. The nurses
15 would patch them up
send them back out
to the front

But they would come back
in their hundreds it
20 seemed.
The bell rang.

I don't quite know when
the war began
I'm sure I don't know
25 how.
But the end I still remember
now.

I don't want her patching
me up, one of the soldiers
30 said

Why? said one of the other
nurses.
She's black, he said.
She's black, the nurse heard.
35 She's black and I cried

I walked away, the other
nurse she came with me
Never mind, she said
reassuringly
40 We'll find something
new.

But even then we both knew
Playtimes would never be
the same.

Theatre review: *Richard III*

John Thaxter, The Stage

In this review, from *The Stage* magazine, John Thaxter looks at a
production of William Shakespeare's *Richard III* at the Globe Theatre
in London. As you read it, think about the way in which the review is
structured and the various elements he has covered within it, as well
as the opinion, if any, the reviewer has of the production. Use the
activities on pages 178–179 to help you.

Barry Kyle's revival makes theatre history as the play's first all-
female production on a major professional stage.

The newly-formed Women's Company rises to the occasion, led
with gleeful but soft-spoken wickedness by Kathryn Hunter who,
5 although rejecting both hump and leg-iron, rivals **Tony Sher**'s
famous 'bottled spider', nimbly prancing on one-legged tiptoe, a
withered arm in a black leather glove. But putting her personal
stamp on the role she clearly imports some aspects of Richard's
character from the *Henry VI* prequel, a villain determined to
10 'catch the crown' through smiles and murder.

The play is also notable for its powerful mafia of grieving widows
effectively drawing the spotlight away from Richard in the second
half. Particularly awesome is the debate between Penelope
Dimond as Richard's mother, Linda Bassett powerfully angry as
15 the ancient Queen Margaret, and Yolanda Vazquez as Edward's
widowed queen, not to mention Meredith MacNeill, rouged and
powdered as Lady Anne, object of Richard's lust.

The principal beneficiaries of **cross-casting** are Amanda Harris as
a powerful Buckingham, a spindoctor rallying the London mob,

Tony Sher   (Sir) Anthony Sher – actor famous for his performance as
Richard III
cross-casting   women playing men's roles, or men playing women's roles.

---

and Louise Bush as Richmond, founder of a new Tudor dynasty, both clearly relishing this rare opportunity to play stirring masculine roles.

Costumes by Jenny Tiramani reflect the period of the play, while much of the macho drive is developed through drum-based music, contrasted with medieval Cypriot chorales for the laments.

The Bosworth battle, preceded by a ghostly parade of Richard's bloodied victims, is too tentative until the final clash of steel between Richard and Richmond. But the military choreography is crisply done and leads effectively into a spirited Globe dance of triumph for the whole company.

Come On Baby, Light My Fire!

Dominic Francis

This review, taken from the National Theatre's website, is really an introduction to a company called Fireraisers, who have performed at the National Theatre, as a way of letting readers know what they can expect from this company. To this extent, you might wish to consider how much this is a review, and how much it is a form of advertising for the company/theatre. Use the activities on pages 180–181 to help you.

Motorbikers, jet skiers, sky divers … I'm not talking about the next James Bond film, they all featured in a spectacular multimedia performance called *This Rough Magic* on Brighton Beach last summer. Based on *The Tempest*, with a cast of over a
5 hundred, it was the most ambitious project to date by Fireraisers, a performance company described by the *Guardian* as 'One of the great hopes for modern British theatre.'

Formed in 1995 by Polly Wiseman and Anton Binder, its main aim is, 'To re-invent live performance for the twenty-first century.'
10 Fireraisers' shows combine traditional theatrical elements, such as writers and actors, with the very latest in techno-wizardry, including video-projections, pyrotechnics and digital animation. 'Now that all this technology exists,' Polly explains, 'you have to consider it as another tool that you can use.'

15 Previous productions have taken place in a variety of venues, from West End theatres to nightclubs and shop windows. For the show in Brighton, the company towed an oil rig all the way from Newhaven and dumped it on the beach. 'There were so many rumours,' laughs Polly. 'People thought an alien spaceship had
20 landed!'

The use of unusual performance spaces, stunning visuals and kicking drum and bass soundtracks is all part of the company's

---

answer to the problem of dwindling theatre audiences, particularly among young people. 'I'm not really sure the solution
25 is to do plays about "youth" subjects,' says Polly. 'I think you have to break down the stigma about going into this building that calls itself a theatre. That's why we do a lot of site-specific stuff.'

It certainly seems to be working. *This Rough Magic* attracted a record audience – for a performance art piece – of over 40,000
30 people. With nominations for theatre awards, glowing reviews in the press and the support of such theatrical heavyweights as Richard Attenborough, Fireraisers are going from strength to strength.

Their next show *Killing Kittens* continues the policy of making
35 innovative and creative use of modern technology, as the company look ahead to the next century by re-examining some of the famous icons of the last. As they state in their manifesto, 'Theatre needs to take a completely new direction if it is to survive in the new millennium.'

40 With Fireraisers on board, I'm sure it will.

Film review: *Drive Me Crazy*

From IOFilm website by The Wolf

Film reviews serve a similar function to theatre reviews – to give you a glimpse of the storyline, and key moments; to provide a flavour of the style of what has been seen; and to offer a view on how good the performances are, and the overall effect and success of the production (or in this case, film). This review is of the Hollywood 'teen romance' *Drive Me Crazy* from a film website. Read the review then complete the activities on pages 182–183.

The social strata of high school life provide endless fodder for moviemakers and psychiatrists. *Drive Me Crazy* succumbs to some obvious clichés, but for the most part is an original, funny tale of love and **angst** in teenage America.

5 In this witty update of the **Pygmalion** story, popular Nicole Maris (Melissa Joan Hart) makes over her beatnik neighbour Chase Hammond (Adrian Grenier) when the pair decide to pretend a love affair to make their true crushes jealous. Of course, it never goes according to plan, and the two kids from different worlds
10 are drawn to each other.

Hart shows natural comic timing. She wins our heart with her manoeuverings and take-charge attitude, not to mention a kindness not often seen in the teenage set. Of course, the splay of freckles and adolescent baby fat don't hurt.

15 Grenier displays an effortless charisma that makes it entirely believable the athletic in-crowd would accept him as one of their own. The pair play off each other nicely, creating good chemistry.

The production is nothing to speak of, with shots of a high school that could have been filmed anytime in the last two decades. But

---

angst   self-doubt/worry
Pygmalion   Greek myth behind *My Fair Lady*, in which an uneducated working-class girl is transformed into a social success

---

20 director John Schultz's clever cuts and a brisk pace keep our interest.

Screenwriter Rob Thomas certainly knows his stuff, as he intersperses clever banter with pop-culture references and the identifying marks of the different social sets. Nicole accuses Chase
25 of a fondness for clove cigarettes and bongos, even as he promises to stop by the mall for a Swatch.

At times the story is heavy-handed. Nicole's distrust of the male sex stems from her father being unreliable, natch. This is resolved in a saccharine way, as all the loose ends get tied up in the last 20
30 minutes.

Though the messages aren't new, they're delivered in a quick-witted, charming way. We're fond of Nicole and Chase so it makes sense they're fond of each other.

And even their agreement to fake a romance makes sense. In a
35 world where fathers leave and mothers die, a business arrangement can seem the safest way to love.

In the end, neither these hardened teens nor the audience is immune to love. You won't be surprised by this film's destination, but it's an entertaining ride.

Playing a leading character

Barnaby Kay

In this interview, actor Barnaby Kay describes how he approached the part of Banquo in William Shakespeare's *Macbeth*. Banquo is Macbeth's best friend (or appears to be) at the start of the play, but when he refuses to go along with Macbeth's murderous plans, Macbeth has him killed. However, his son, Fleance, manages to escape. Read this interview then complete the activities on page 184.

'It will be rain tonight': Barnaby Kay ponders Banquo's fate

Barnaby Kay last worked with the director, Ed Hall, eight years ago, when Ed was an assistant director with the Royal Shakespeare Company. Barnaby is considerably younger than
5 most actors who are cast as Banquo.

How are you playing Banquo?

The traditional view of Banquo is that he's the opposite of Macbeth – that Macbeth becomes all that is evil and Banquo is all that is good – but I didn't want to play him like that. He's a warrior just
10 like Macbeth, a killer of men. Given that I'm young for the part, I'm playing him as a general who has risen quickly through the ranks and is able to command the respect of his elders. In his **soliloquy** Banquo wishes the Weird Sisters' prophesies to work for him as they have for Macbeth (*'may they not ... set me up in hope?'*) so it's
15 by no means cut and dried where Banquo's ambition might take him. In our production the soliloquy comes at the end of the first half so the audience leave for the interval not sure what Banquo might do to Macbeth on his arrival in Scone.

What have you discovered about Banquo's relationship with
20 **nature?**

Banquo looks upon nature at various times in the play and sees a

---

soliloquy speech given by a character on his or her own, often revealing innermost feelings

---

deeper meaning. When he arrives at Macbeth's castle, a place he would have known very well, he is struck by the abundance of house martins nesting there (*'this bird hath made his procreant*
25 *cradle'*). They have taken on a darker significance, becoming almost like crows circling the castle. When his son, Fleance, wakes from a nightmare Banquo notices that there are no stars in the sky (*'the candles are all out'*) so in trying to calm the boy down he's also trying to calm himself, clutching the boy for comfort.

30 On the night of his death Banquo notices the signs of a storm and sees this as another prophesy. *'It will be rain tonight'* is the last thing he says before he is murdered and in this production he's holding Fleance's hand as they look out towards the sky together.

What is Banquo's relationship with Macbeth?
35 He is already feeling uneasy when Macbeth enters the scene with Fleance. As the lights cut out, Banquo inadvertently draws a knife on his friend but when the lights return the tension remains. Macbeth promises reward for Banquo (*'if you shall cleave to my consent'*) and in this moment the friendship is finished. Banquo
40 knows then that Macbeth has ambitions to make himself King, to fulfil the prophesy one way or another, and this is what separates their personalities – just how far Macbeth is prepared to go. Duncan is killed that night and when Macbeth confesses to killing the murderers (*'yet I do repent me ... that I did kill them'*)
45 Banquo is certain Macbeth has taken the step he feared.

When do you think Macbeth decides to murder Banquo?
It is Banquo's attitude before the banquet that actually decides his fate. Macbeth is testing him while asking apparently straightforward questions (*'is't far you ride?'*) but Banquo's
50 answers are deliberately flippant (*'as far as will fill up the time ...'*). He's making it clear their friendship is over, that they have nothing more to say to each other. In our playing of the scene Banquo's sarcasm encourages the court to laugh with him and this 'winds up' Macbeth to such an extent that he decides to

55 murder both Banquo and his son that night. There is a false exit for Banquo when Macbeth stops him on a **half-line** with *'goes Fleance with you?'* and he realises at that moment that his son is in danger.

How are you playing the ghost?

60 The ghost is Banquo at his purest with all his ability to gloss and keep things hidden stripped away. He is very conscious and knows exactly what he is doing to Macbeth; it's his revenge. There's a moment in our staging where the ghost gets up to leave while Macbeth is saying to him *'If thou canst nod speak too'* at which

65 point the ghost spins on him as if to say: 'Are you challenging me to talk? Do you <u>really</u> want me to speak to you?' An idea from rehearsals which may not be kept in the show is that we see Macbeth's victims living as ghosts in his everyday life throughout the second half. If Banquo's ghost stays onstage he will have a look

70 on his face as if to say: 'I'm here to stay – I'm always going to be a part of your life because of what you've done.'

---

half-line   a line of dialogue that is only half of a normal verse line and usually signals an interruption

---

Alfie Moon interviewed

Actor Shane Richie on EastEnders *website*

Sometimes the links between who you are and the part you are playing can be huge, especially if you are one of the leading characters in the most watched soap in the country. In this interview Shane Richie, who plays Alfie Moon in *EastEnders*, describes how he got the part, and what it's like playing Alfie. As you read, think about how you can incorporate elements of your own character into your acting. Use the activities on page 185 to help you.

How have your first months on the show been?
The first few months are a bit like a honeymoon. The first episode is like the wedding. Then comes the stage when you're trying to find your way around and develop your own routine.
5 I'll have been here a year in September, so the honeymoon's coming to an end. I've moved into the house, become part of the furniture and Shane and Alfie are taking each other for granted!

Did you expect such a fantastic reaction from the public?
10 I arrived on the show with a reputation. I wasn't an unknown, so I knew that people would love or hate me. I'd filmed 20 episodes before I was seen on screen.

I watched the first episode at home and was petrified. The following day, I came into work and the reaction from the cast
15 and public was fantastic. It was such a weight off my shoulders. I could just enjoy what I was doing after that.

Have you had any input into the character?
I wasn't keen on the name Alfie at first, but now I can't imagine him being anything else. Originally, he was going to be Alfie
20 Carter and I loved all the Michael Caine connotations. When I heard it would be Moon, I sneered.

His clothes had a lot to do with me. He's based on **Tony Jordan**, the creator of the Slaters and many of the great characters. He wears jeans, cowboy boots and **lairy** shirts. It's a bit of a thank you to him really.

Is your dress sense similar?
He's destroyed my wardrobe! I've got a long leather coat that I've had to put back in the cupboard. I can't wear it anymore, even though it cost me loads. If I put it on people assume that I'm filming. I like to wear jeans and boots like Alfie, but not really the shirts.

How were you cast in the show?
I originally auditioned for Tom. After the workshop, they saw me improvise and they liked that. I suppose I played myself, a bit of a cheeky chap.

How was the Moon family created?
I auditioned with several young actors to play Spencer, but Chris Parker was by far the best. They wanted someone who brought an innocence to the show. Chris does that brilliantly.

As soon as I found out that Hilda Braid would be Nana, I was bowled over. The body of experience that she brings to the show is amazing. I knew that the family was really well cast.

Do you have a good bond off-screen too?
Oh yes. I'm like the big brother Chris never had. He phones me several times a day. I've never had a nan, so I call Hilda 'Nana' off-screen too.

What did you think of Alfie's dramatic introduction?
It was all very well them writing a new character for me, but for him to take over the Vic in his first episode was a very brave

---

Tony Jordan story consultant and leading writer for *EastEnders* (see his Kat/Zoe script on pages 50–53)
lairy bright, over the top

move. I was happy to do it, but it could have blown up in the writers' faces.

What have been your favourite scenes so far?
I love my entrance – the whole **blag**. Kat and Alfie's on-off relationship has been good. I've actually just filmed my favourite scene. It's with Nana, and I absolutely adore it.

Do you find it harder to do the emotional rather than comedy scenes?
No, funnily enough. Alfie can be very upbeat and comic, but it's a fantastic relief to get the emotionally heavy scenes. It stretches me as an actor. The analogy I make is with David Jason. For years he made us laugh as Del Boy, but he did that one scene when he became a father and made us cry. I'd love to think that Alfie could have that appeal. As an actor, you need to have your emotions at your fingertips.

How did you and Jessie work on the chemistry between Kat and Alfie?
We have a lot of fun together off-screen and are both volatile. We're very honest with each other and have rowed. When someone's that honest with you, you trust them. As actors, that's worth its weight in gold.

Are you that glad Alfie and Kat have finally got together?
Oh yes. There's some fantastic stuff coming up. We can't believe what we read in the scripts. It will never be plain sailing between them. Someone's always going to throw a cat amongst the pigeons.

Were you a fan of the show before you joined?
I knew a lot of the cast. I appeared in *Grease* with Tamzin Outhwaite (Mel). I knew Natalie Cassidy and Barbara Windsor. I worked with Ricky Groves in *Burnside*. I remember him telling me that he was going for a part in *EastEnders*!

---

blag   bluff or con

---

80   I watched it when I could, but I was always touring so didn't catch it all the time

How did you get into acting initially?
I started off in local theatre and then worked in **Rep**. I didn't have formal training.

85 **What advice would you give aspiring actors?**
Think carefully! 99% of actors are out of work at some time. I'm fortunate that I've never been out of work because I've done musical theatre, presenting and so on. I've enjoyed doing everything, but some people just want to act. I'm at my happiest
90   now though. I've found my vocation!

You're involved in a new film aren't you?
Yes, *Shoreditch*. It's due to premiere in November. Myself and Joely Richardson star in it. My friend wrote it and I'm involved in the production. I filmed it before I began *EastEnders*. My
95   character's very different to Alfie. He's very dark and says very little. I'd like to do another film if it stretched me as an actor.

Do you miss performing in front of a live audience?
I went to see *The Rat Pack* the other night and for the first time since I joined *EastEnders*, I wanted to be on the stage. It's the
100   immediate reaction from the audience. Whether it's musical theatre, stand-up comedy or in my band – you only have one shot at getting it right. Here, if I go wrong we cut and retake.

How do you like to spend any spare time?
Recently, I've caught up on a few West End shows. I love them.
105   Basically, I'm really enjoying my personal life at the moment and love spending time at home. I like watching movies. Plus, I've been writing my autobiography.

What do your kids think about you being on the show?
Dad's cool now! My boy's even asked for a leather coat which

Rep   repertory company

110 made me laugh. Jessie and I are presenting Party in the Park this
     year too. Credibility doesn't pay the mortgage though, but it is
     nice!

Is it true that your nickname is 'Charlie Big Potatoes'?
Yes, that's what Steve McFadden called me when I first joined the
115 show. It's because Alfie runs the Vic.

The audience booed!

Holly Harris

In this piece, Holly Harris, a 14-year-old student, describes what it was like preparing for a lead role in her school musical, and evaluates her performance. As you read, consider the extent to which you are able to comment in the same way on performances, or other stage work, of your own. Is there anything she has left out? Anything that is not sufficiently explained? But, most importantly, do you get a sense of what *process* she went through and the skills involved? Use the activities on page 186 to help you.

I suppose you can split the experience into two parts – all the time rehearsing and preparing, and then the actual performances, which only lasted three nights, after months of rehearsals! Even now it's difficult to believe I did it, but it must be true as the
5 photos are all around school, and people still talk to me about it.

Basically, I played the character called Cyndi, in a musical called *Back to the 80s*. It was a little like *Grease*, but set in the 80s, with songs from the 80s. My character spends most of her time telling guys they're not good enough for her, or destroying their fragile
10 egos. Her key song – and big number/dance routine is 'Material Girl', by Madonna. This sums Cyndi up: her motivation is money and glamour.

Playing Cyndi didn't come naturally to me, though I enjoyed the part. It's always good playing nasty parts – they get all the good
15 lines. When I delivered my 'put-downs' to one of the boys, the audience booed me! I suppose I should have been pleased, but it was kind of a shock. It just goes to show that you can't predict an audience's reactions. Funnily enough, that was on the first night. The second and third night, they didn't boo, and I was almost
20 disappointed.

So how did I go about playing Cyndi? I guess the key to her was the 'withering looks' she gave to other characters, especially boys.

I tried to literally 'look down my nose' at those I despised. I would place my hands on my hips and stare at them sideways, almost with my back to them, as if to say 'you're not worth my full attention.' It seemed to work, especially on the first and second nights, though perhaps I didn't have quite the same energy, or something, on the last night. Who knows? It's difficult to put your finger on why something works one night and not on another.

The make-up and costume definitely helped me develop the character. I'm not saying I didn't feel like Cyndi before the dress rehearsal, but the process of going out to shops and trying to find suitable Cyndi-style gear helped me get into the part. With each small accessory I bought – from the lurid yellow tights to the groovy pink hooped earrings – I felt like I was becoming more like this real person, not just a girl who has some lines in the play.

The most difficult parts of the performance weren't the lines or the acting, really. I felt pretty ok about all that. No, it was the dancing and the singing. I've had a lot of singing experience, though not in shows, but the dancing was something else – especially when you had to sing at the same time. I was conscious of the radio mic and wondered if it was working – which it wasn't in the dress rehearsal! Fortunately, on the actual night it worked fine.

The musical was supposed to be pretty energetic and physical. All the songs, just about, involved leaping about over furniture, or swinging people round, and you realise just how physically fit and active you have to be in shows like these. I was exhausted at the end, both physically and mentally – but on a real high. After the show had finished I felt so down – almost like I'd suffered bereavement. I behaved like a real showbiz type, mooching around my house with a depressed look on my face. Ah, the price of fame!

Although it's very difficult to judge when you're on stage how good the overall performances are, the reactions we got were brilliant – and, in a way, the mistakes we made didn't matter. It was all part of the live theatre experience.

All-in-all, I'm sad to leave Cyndi behind, even if she was a right cow! And I'm sad to leave the 'team' behind, because it really is a team effort. When you hear actors and actresses at awards ceremonies bleating on about thanking this person or that
60 person, or director X or producer Y, you think – oh, stop being a luvvie and get on with it! But it's true. Everyone works together when they're performing, and it is a team.

If that makes me a luvvie then so be it!

Work in progress

Jan Smith

In this piece, Jan Smith, a student in Year 9, describes how he and the rest of his group took a poem, 'The Listeners', by Walter de la Mare, and turned it into a polished improvisation, *The Traveller*. (You can read a transcript of part of his group's performance on pages 11–14). As you read, consider how well (or badly) Jan has tracked the development of the ideas. Think too, about whether his group's way of working reflects yours, and what you can learn from his experience. Use the activities on pages 187–189 to help you.

First of all our teacher read us this poem called 'The Listeners', which most of us didn't really understand, but we were told to use it just as a 'stimulus' or 'springboard' for our ideas. I think this meant that we didn't have to sort of take it word-for-word or
5 make a story of the poem but we could just pick up on anything that stood out and take it from there.

Then our teacher told us to pick one 'powerful line' from the poem, so our group went for *'phantom listeners'*. We were then told to make some sort of shape or frozen tableau relating to
10 the line.

We messed around a bit for a few minutes, and basically just made some ghost shapes – like hands held in the air and creepy looks on our faces. Then we saw what other groups had done, and ours looked a bit pathetic to be honest. Basically, when we evaluated
15 what we'd done, it wasn't that good. We'd just sort of done a cliché of what ghosts were like. So, we started discussing phantoms and wondered if they were like real people – perhaps they even wanted to be part of the world, but couldn't (that was Ali's idea, actually).

20 So, next we had to look at the poem again, and decide if we could make a story of some sort. We were still thinking about the

phantom idea, but realised it needed to be original, or everybody would just be bored rigid.

25 Then, I think it was Daniel suggested we should have this phantom person – or people – in the house when the traveller calls, but the phantom family aren't frightening, they are frightened and that's why they don't answer at first.

We stood up and tried it out. I was the traveller, so I crept up to this imaginary house and door and knocked on it, and asked if
30 anybody was in. Then Ali answered, I think as a joke at first, 'Nobody's here!' which made us all kill ourselves laughing, but when we'd got over it this seemed like a really good concept. I mean, who would be stupid enough to shout 'nobody'?

That's when Sean said it could be a kid. 'Cos they wouldn't think
35 before answering – or they might have been told not to answer but couldn't stop themselves from saying something. And that was when we realised we'd got an idea – or the basis of one. The people inside want to be found – and don't want to be found. They're lonely because of something they have done that won't
40 allow them to live in the real world.

At this point, we all stopped and quickly made some notes of our ideas before we forgot everything.

Then, we stood up again, and tried to improvise a scene. We started with me hammering on the door and Ali answering. But
45 we decided to use darkness and light by having him answer from 'off stage' as if he was hiding something at first. Then Ali said perhaps the child might have an illness, like the plague, or something. And Daniel suggested it could be something that left a mark or scar, and that was why he wouldn't be seen.

50 We then had to show a sort of halfway point freeze-frame, so we had me hammering on the door, and Ali right to the side holding, or hiding his face. And then, just because they weren't doing something, Daniel stood at the side, near Ali, watching him – like

a father or something, and Sean stood behind me, crouching, like he was my servant.

This was really where our presentation of *The Traveller* started, and everything we did after this was based on this concept. Our intention was to make something chilling, but not too like other things people had seen. You will have to judge for yourself if you see the final piece whether we succeeded.

Activities

Black Truth (page 154)

It's important in your work in drama that at some point you consider the role 'play' and drama have in our lives. After all, whether we're playing mummies and daddies in the playground at primary school, watching *EastEnders* or booing at the local pantomime, it's clear that drama – in all its forms – remains central to our lives.

Making: writing about play

1. In 'Black Truth' on pages 154–155 Brenda Agard describes 'play-acting' as if it were real.

- What 'game' is being played?
- When do we realise that it is a children's game?
- Are there any earlier clues?

2. Is the poem being told through the eyes of the child as it happened, or is the poet looking back as an older person? Or a mixture of the two?

   Can you find evidence for your views?

3. Write about your own experiences of 'play' in all its forms from when you were a young child. Include in your account the following things:

- your first memories of 'play-acting' (i.e. pretending to be someone else – on your own or with friends; playground games; songs, etc.)
- particular events or occasions when you 'became' someone else (e.g. fancy-dress parties, early school plays or performances, acting or performing for parents or friends at home)
- your view of 'play' now: do you still like to dress up, become someone else, show off – or are you not a natural performer? Do you enjoy drama at school – or do you find it too embarrassing?

Who do you think in your own class is a 'good actor'? What do you think makes them so good?

Responding

Choose a moment from your childhood (either playing games at school, or an occasion where you had to act or dress up) and write a poem or a monologue as your older self looking back. You could start: '*I remember...*'

Theatre review: *Richard III* (page 156)

Making: writing about a performer

Watching a performance and observing the quality of the performances, the interpretation of the play, and still being able to say something about the story takes real skill. Look at the first paragraph from John Thaxter's review on page 156, and the annotations around it:

Comment on actress's interpretation of role	Praises the production	Name of actress playing lead role

The newly-formed Women's Company **rises to the occasion**, led with gleeful but **soft-spoken wickedness** by **Kathryn Hunter** who, although rejecting both hump and leg-iron, **rivals Tony Sher's** famous 'bottled spider', nimbly prancing on one-legged tiptoe, a **withered arm in a black leather glove**. But putting her personal stamp on the role she clearly imports some aspects of Richard's character from the *Henry VI* prequel, a villain determined to **'catch the crown'** through smiles and murder.

Quotation from the play to support the way the actress has chosen to play part	Specific reference to how she looks	Refers to another production

Write your own paragraph or two about *one person* you have seen perform recently. You will not be able to include all the things John Thaxter does, but try to include the following:

- the name of the actor/actress concerned
- a detail about his/her appearance (especially if costume is used)
- a couple of appropriate character descriptions (i.e. noun phrases such as 'soft-spoken wickedness')
- use of the present tense
- an indication of your view of the performance (play and/or performer).

Responding

When you have written this first paragraph, go back to John Thaxter's review on pages 156–157, and list the other elements he has covered. Can you see any *critical* elements in his review?

Come On Baby, Light My Fire! (page 158)

Writing about performances you have seen generally involves trying to create a picture in the reader's mind about what you saw. The reader, of course, hasn't usually seen the production, so your task is to give a *flavour* of what it was like, but with accurate factual information. It's no good saying that there was a flying car in the production if there wasn't!

Making

1. Describe to a friend any TV show or film that you have seen but they haven't. Your description should last no longer than one minute and should cover: who was in it, the basic storyline or content, and the 'feel' of the show.

   Afterwards, check whether they felt you gave them a good sense of what the film or programme was like.

2. Now re-read the review/article about the show *This Rough Magic* on pages 158–159. What has Dominic Francis covered? Find examples of the following:

- name of the company and its founders
- key elements of their productions
- quotations from the founders
- praise for the company and its productions from the writer and others.

Responding

Now write your own review, in this style, of any performance or production you have seen either in class or outside. If you want to, you can make up the review – the key thing is to include some of the features Dominic Francis uses – and bear in mind that this is more like an advertisement or promotional piece than a traditional review.

You could start:

Powerful acting, fantastic use of school uniform, and clever use of classroom tables and chairs characterised the performance of group 3 in my drama class. As Danny explains, 'We really tried to make an impact …', etc.

Try to include a range of 'theatre words' in your review, such as:

staging; movement; use of space; dialogue; convention; gesture; impact; power; characterisation; tension; dramatic effect, etc.

Drive Me Crazy (page 160)

Making

Reviews, as you have seen, are made up of a range of elements, such as:

- plot/story/content details
- brief character/actor descriptions: looks, behaviour, etc.
- set/production details: tone/style, overall effect, etc.
- audience/reviewer response – good, bad, indifferent.

1. The first element is not as straightforward as it looks. How do you condense two or three hours' action into a few lines? Let's look at the *Drive Me Crazy* review on pages 160–161. The table below shows some examples of writing about the plot.

'... an original, funny tale of love and angst in teenage America ...'	Here, the reviewer highlights **key themes** and the **location**
'... witty update of the Pygmalion story ...'	Refers to **another story** the film is loosely based on
'... the pair decide to pretend a love affair to make their true crushes jealous. Of course, it never goes according to plan, and the two kids from different worlds are drawn to each other ...'	**Actual details** of the story itself, condensed into a few lines
'... Nicole's distrust of the male sex stems from her father being unreliable, natch. This is resolved in a saccharine way, as all the loose ends get tied up in the last 20 minutes ...'	**Explanation** of the story and **why a character behaves as she does,** plus reference to **how story ends** (without saying exactly what happens)

2. Find any other examples of what actually happens in the story.

Responding

Now, practise the skill of summarising a storyline in a few, well-chosen sentences. Here is an example of a one-line summary of a famous play:

Romeo and Juliet: a tragic tale of romantic obsession set against a backdrop of warring familes in 16th-century Verona.

Choose any well-known story, film or play (or a production/ performance you have been involved in) and sum it up in a single line, like this. Then write a 150-word explanation of the plot and what happens.

Playing a leading character (page 162)

Commenting on your own performance in a production is difficult. After all, you were performing, so how can you observe how well you did? Perhaps, like Barnaby Kay, it is better to comment on how you played the part – and what you were trying to achieve.

Making

Look again at Barnaby Kay's account of playing Banquo on pages 162–164.

- How does he go against the 'traditional' way of playing Banquo?
- Barnaby Kay talks about Banquo's answers and actions as if Shakespeare had included them in the play – but these are actually interpretations. Find the section where he mentions how Banquo is sarcastic. Why has Barnaby chosen to do this in the play?
- Barnaby Kay also refers to the rehearsal process and one quite ambitious idea that they considered using. What was that idea?

Responding

Over a period of time, keep a rehearsal journal in which you make notes on the ways a character you are playing progresses. Consider:

How you first saw the character and why.	e.g. *I thought my character was bold and fearless, but ...*
What you introduced into your way of playing him or her to create a particular effect or impact.	e.g. *I decided my character had fear deep inside, so I decided that she would constantly fiddle with her rosary beads.*
How the final performance of your character went – make close reference to how you say individual lines, gestures you make, and your relationship to other characters.	e.g. *I wanted to show the gulf between me and my husband, so I always stood on the other side of the table, clutching the edge for support.*

Alfie Moon interviewed (page 165)

Shows such as *EastEnders* often try out different combinations of actors before they make final casting decisions, and this seems to be the case with Shane Richie, who says he '... originally auditioned for Tom' (a boyfriend of the character, Sharon).

Making

1. In your group, select a short scene that involves a minimum of three or four characters (perhaps one from this book). Each of you should take a character to prepare. One member of the group should *not* take a role, but should be the director.

    Think about what you as a person can bring to the role. If you are naturally shy, would that suit your character? If so, how can you make use of that element of your personality?

    Now, audition for your role. You can either take a speech by your character, or, better still, perform a section with one or two other characters.

2. After the 'audition' has finished, make brief notes on how you did – and, importantly, what you felt the 'chemistry' was like between you and the others you auditioned with.

3. Then, swap roles within the group, and go through the audition again. When you have finished, make notes again on how you and the others performed.

4. Finally, let the director give his or her opinion on who has been selected for each part. Are you pleased with your part? Did it fit in with what you felt about your own performance?

Responding

Looking through what Shane Richie says on pages 165–169, what do you think he feels are the main reasons why his character has been so successful?

For example, is it because he is playing a character who is utterly different from him? Or because he is very like Alfie? What other reasons do you think made the character work?

The audience booed! (page 170)

Holly Harris's experiences of performing are a pretty good model of how you might write about your own performances or stage work. The work comes across as personal, yet reasonably well-informed, but how would you go about writing a similar commentary? First, look at how her piece was constructed.

Making

Here are *two* of the features of her commentary, with examples:

General details about the show: *It was a little like* Grease, *but set in the 80s*

The audience reaction: *When I delivered my 'put-downs' to one of the boys, the audience booed me!*

Can you now find examples of these other features? Find relevant quotations from pages 170–172 and note them down:

- specific details about how Holly played Cyndi
- technical and practical issues related to the performance
- how she related to the character, and how she got 'into the part'
- her views about who was responsible for the success of the show
- her emotions and feelings once the show had ended.

Performing and responding

Using the same basic paragraph structure as Holly's, write a commentary on a show you have been in (it doesn't have to be a leading role). Divide your account into paragraphs covering each of the features above.

- try to give a sense of the *overall effect* of the performance on you and the audience

- be as *precise as you can* about *specific decisions* you made (or that were suggested to you) about the way to play your character. For example, gestures, ways of speaking, moving – the choice of costume (if you had a costume), etc.

Work in progress (page 173)

Jan Smith's account is a little rough around the edges. It was written as he progressed, and features some quite informal language (e.g. 'sort of done') but this is fine for an ongoing commentary. The key thing here is to use the commentary as a way of improving your own work. In Jan Smith's case, he learns how an idea can evolve, and the exercises below are designed to show you how you might learn from his experience.

1. Jan says his group's initial work was unsatisfactory because they had '... just sort of done a cliché of what ghosts were like' (page 173). What does he mean by this?

2. Now, with a partner, look at the idea chart below, based on the word 'phantom'.

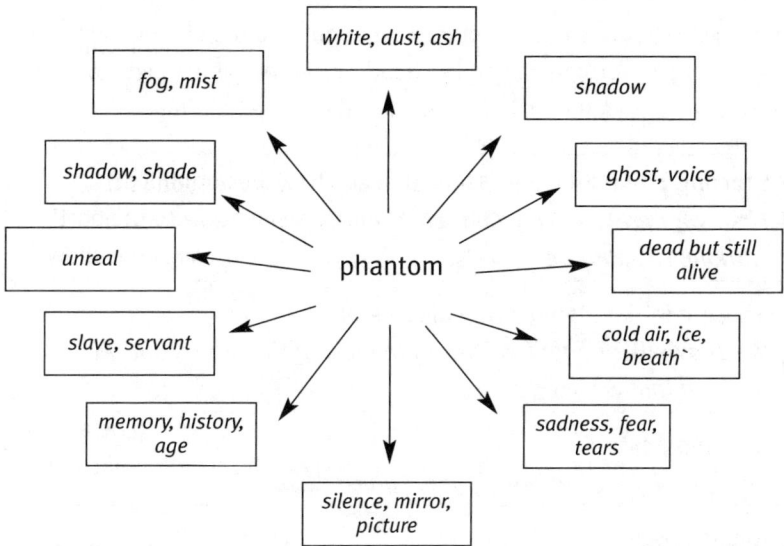

Some of these ideas are direct noun responses to the word – i.e. 'phantom' – 'ghost', 'shadow', but others are adjectives such as 'unreal'; others are more to do with a feeling the word creates (e.g. 'dust', 'ice', 'age', etc.).

Making

1. In pairs, take two of these boxes and develop a short dialogue in which a phantom speaks. In his or her first line, he or she must use the phrase 'I am ...' plus some or all of the words in the box, and then elaborate further, e.g.

   PHANTOM　　*I am silence. A mirror. I watch you every day in your pretty little room. My room ...*

2. Next, take this starting point and develop from it a drama based on these opening words. You may wish to join up with other pairs to share your dialogues before deciding where your drama takes you. The final piece can be as short – or as long – as you like. The only rule is that you try to avoid 'cliché' – that is, try to make your drama original.

However, as you work, you must keep regular notes of your own – and your group's – progress. Use the headings in the table below to help you, or invent your own headings, if that is more helpful.

Starting points (the initial stimulus and how we responded) *First, we were given an ideas chart for the word 'phantom'. Then, working in pairs, we ...*
Sharing initial ideas/group discussion *We showed our opening lines to the rest of the group, and we decided that we liked ...*
Developments *Then, we took the opening line, and created ...*
In performance *Our final presentation consisted of ...*
Evaluation *Looking back, I think certain elements worked, such as ...*

Responding

Once you have finished both your performance and your ongoing commentary, turn the account into a continuous piece of prose like Jan's (without headings).

- Have you given as good a sense of the development of the work as he has?
- If not, what have you missed?
- Are there things about Jan's that he could have improved? For example, is it too chatty? Does it give enough detail on how the work progressed?

Development and extension

The language of drama

Any commentary or evaluation of how you played a particular role, is dependent on you having at your fingertips the appropriate vocabulary to describe the processes of rehearsal and performance.

Look at these two extracts from accounts by students:

Student A

Well, I thought the acting wasn't very good. I mean she didn't really play the part very well and her movements were not very believable. Especially with her husband.

Student B

I found her acting unconvincing. At one point, she stood downstage with her back to her husband, with her arms crossed. Was this the action of a woman who was tender and sympathetic?

What is better about the second example? Consider:

- the use of adjectives to describe character and performance
- how well the comments focus on the skills used by the actress
- the expression of ideas: is one too chatty? Or too formal?

Having appropriate language related to the theatre is useful as it takes away some of the vagueness of the first response, and enables people who read your work to see how you think about and understand dramatic work.

Comparing language

Of course, technical language isn't enough – and as you have seen in this section, crisp and relevant phrases about characters and storylines also help.

Compare the ways John Thaxter and Barnaby Kay talk about Shakespearean characters in their articles about *Richard III* and Banquo. Copy and complete the table on the next page.

Features	*Richard III*	*Macbeth*
Interpretation of play	*'all-female production'* *'cross-casting'* *'powerful mafia of grieving widows'*	Nothing in particular
Characters and how they act	Richard: Buckingham:	Banquo: '... *a general who has risen quickly through the ranks ...'*; Banquo's ghost: '... *The ghost is Banquo at his purest with all his ability to gloss and keep things hidden stripped away ...'*
Moments in the production	Bosworth battle: '... *too tentative until the final clash of steel'*	Banquo and Fleance on their last night together

Once you have completed your table, write a fuller response on the two accounts. What differences and similarities are there between them? Consider:

- the extent to which they give you a sense of how particular characters are played (and the detail provided)
- the different perspectives of reviewer and actor
- the purpose of each piece.

Links to the Framework for Teaching English and key focus

Chapter	Focus	Key drama terms and vocabulary	Main Framework Drama Objectives/ Links to Drama Objectives Bank
1. Collaborations	*Developing improvised, devised and scripted work from a variety of sources*	*improvisation circle dialogue tableau(x) soundscape mini-mime role transcript stress scenario*	Year 7: S&L: 15, 16 Year 8: S&L: 15, 16
2. Repertoires	*A range of scripts designed to develop the full range of drama techniques and skills*	*monologue voice vocal tones stress emphasis space oration ritual levels*	Year 7: S&L: 17, 18 Year 8: S&L: 14 Year 9: S&L: 12, 14
3. Scriptings	*An insight into how scripts are produced by writers, covering the full range from stage to screen*	*empathy transition juxtaposition upstage/ downstage characterisation alienation intention forum theatre dramatic irony scenario*	Year 7: S&L: 16 Year 8: S&L: 16 Year 9: S&L: 14

Chapter	Focus	Key drama terms and vocabulary	Main Framework Drama Objectives/ Links to Drama Objectives Bank
4. Interpretations	*Exploration of how texts and performances create different effects and can be looked at in a range of ways*	*conventions themes evidence protagonist chorus prologue interpretation tradition caricature screenplay*	Year 7: S&L: 18 Year 8: S&L: 16 Year 9: S&L: 13
5. Reflections	*How to write considered and useful analyses and commentaries on drama work*	*cross-casting review company production impact tension audition set location rehearsal perspective*	Year 7: S&L: 19 Year 8: S&L: 13 Year 9: S&L: 11, 15

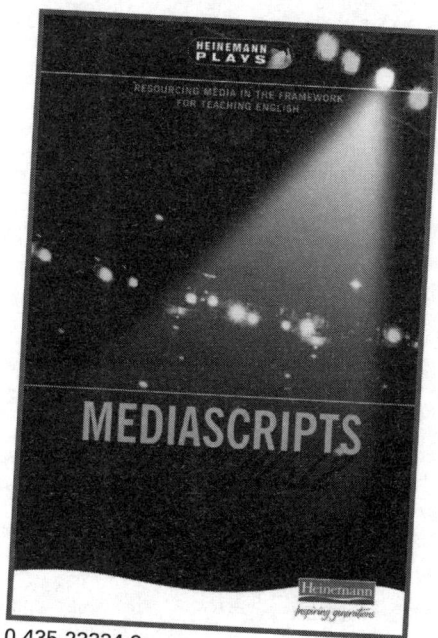

Scenes and Stages

Edited by John O'Connor

Scenes and Stages provides an overview of major plays and playwrights to help meet the drama objectives of the Framework for Teaching English at KS3. It includes:

- extracts written by playwrights suggested in the National Curriculum
- material from different genres, traditions and periods
- sections ranging from Comedy and Mystery to Tragedy and Viewpoints on Society
- activities designed to support the drama objectives.

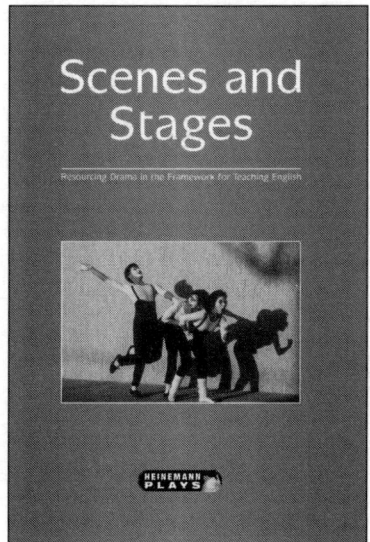

Scenes and
Stages

Resourcing Drama in the Framework for Teaching English

HEINEMANN
PLAYS

0 435 23331 9

Heinemann

Inspiring generations

Scripts and Sketches

Edited by John O'Connor

This stimulating collection of original short plays for Key Stage 3 students is designed for use both in the English and Drama Classrooms. It includes:

- short scripts
- a wide range of genres and styles
- a wide range of dramatic forms and issues
- follow-up activities that support the drama objectives in the Framework for Teaching English

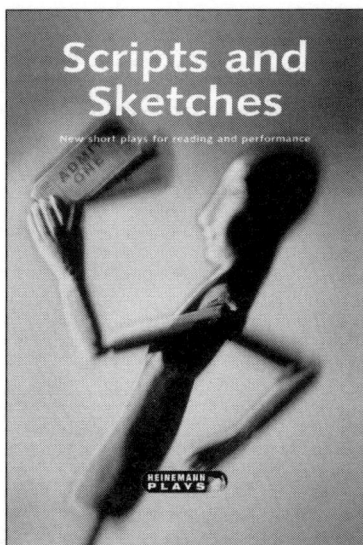

Scripts and Sketches

New short plays for reading and performance

HEINEMANN
PLAYS

0 435 23330 0

Heinemann

Inspiring generations